the long island HOLIDAY COOKBOOK

Newsday
B·O·O·K·S

Dozens of people worked to bring
"The Long Island Holiday Cookbook" to life.
Many thanks are in order, especially to the families who opened their
celebrations to our reporters and photographers.

Printed by Interstate Litho in Brentwood, N.Y.
ISBN:1-885134-25-8

112-6220

introduction

For food writers, perhaps nothing presents a greater challenge than the subject of holidays and food. How to find a fresh approach to holiday fare without shortchanging traditional favorites. We solved our dilemma by turning to the true source of holiday wisdom — the family kitchens of Long Island.

For one year, covering a span of Thanksgiving to Labor Day, our writers and photographers visited home cooks from Montauk to Queens sharing in their family celebrations.

It was a culinary odyssey, filled with discovery as well as comforting traditions. We tasted a delicious Thanksgiving hors d'oeuvre of fried yucca in Dix Hills; a sweet red bean dessert soup for Chinese New Year in Flushing, and steamed seafood straight out of the pit at a Labor Day clambake on the East End. The fare is interesting, even exotic, but the recipes are quite accessible. The result is a guide to the best holiday food on Long Island.

We would like to thank all who opened their houses to us and so graciously shared their treasured recipes:

Carmel and Mario St. Laurent of Dix Hills; Maria Lynn of Lloyd Neck; Lily and Eric Engelhardt of Dix Hills; Michelina and Joseph Cangemi of Hicksville; Tom and Ann Fermature of Massapequa Park; Mildred Clayton of Westbury; Liz and Jimmy Sunshine of Syosset; Jimmy and Shiao-mei Meng of Queens; Jerry and Gloria Landsberg of Great Neck; Joe and Noreen Roughan of Southampton; Chef Matt Kar of Jamesport and Sean Connelly of Laurel; Rev. Robert Newton Terry and the congregants of the Old Steeple Community Church in Aquebogue, and Maureen Tiongco and Harry Theard of Montauk.

contents

THANKSGIVING

Menu

Acra

Potage a l'Oignon With Parmesan Croutons
Roasted Turkey
Pepper Gravy
Ultimate Recipe for Turkey Gravy
Cranberry-Orange Sauce
Garlicked Brussels Sprouts
National Rice
Yams With Apricot Orange Sauce
Potato Stuffing
Corn Bread Dressing

Sweet Potato Pudding
Pumpkin Pie With Ginger Streusel
Pecan Pie

The traditional meal

takes on a Haitian accent

in the hands of five sisters

ABUNDANT BLESSINGS

If it's good to have a sister in the kitchen, Carmel St. Laurent is multiply blessed. She has four sisters with whom she shares the Thanksgiving cooking duties. As a result, she faces the holiday with remarkable grace and composure. That's not to say that it's easy. Among them, the five sisters have 10 children and four husbands — not to mention friends and in-laws. But each sister takes some responsibility for the meal. Ange Joseph of Selden, the oldest, takes care of the turkey. Andre Jean of Deer Park brings a pasta dish. Eddie Adrian of Selden brings dessert, "because she's always the last to arrive," said Carmel, who in turn makes the rice and beans. Edie Joseph, the youngest, makes a good cheesecake and assists any sister who needs help.

As the family sits down to Thanksgiving dinner at Carmel and Mario St. Laurent's Dix Hills home, everyone is mindful of the good things they have and especially of being able to share them with each other. Carmel and her sisters arrived from Haiti in

The sisters, from left, Eddie Adrian and Carmel St. Laurent. Inset, from left, Andre Jean, Edie Joseph and Ange Joseph

1974 and settled in the East New York section of Brooklyn. Over the years, as they grew up, married and had children, they continued to stay near each other. Their 10 children are equally intertwined. "I don't think a month has gone by when we don't all see each other," said Reggie Jean, the oldest cousin. "I'm always surprised everyone else isn't like us."

Mario, a pediatrician who practices in Queens Village and Corona, also grew up in East New York. He remembers leaner times, when the house he and his siblings lived in leaked and when his mother worked two jobs and refused to ask for food stamps. "It was very, very tough," he said, "because of the pride, the Haitian pride. I had to go to school without lunch and sometimes I would pass out. Now I have a better life and I'm trying to make a better life for my children. You have to be thankful for everything you have."

At the St. Laurent house, the Thanksgiving feast begins with a prayer said by the oldest person at both the adult and children's tables. Like the tables of many immigrant families, the St. Laurents' looks like the standard holiday spread at first glance, with a roasted turkey, stuffing, cranberry sauce and vegetables. A closer look reveals some unique flourishes. The stuffing is made with ground beef, potatoes and Jamaican peppers. There is rice and beans, a national Haitian dish. There is fish, usually fried and served with a hot sauce, which, truth be told, the adults prefer to turkey. "The men will pick at the turkey," said Carmel, "but they don't like the white meat. And the cranberry sauce we have for the kids, but we never really acquired a taste for it."

In the end, it's the family gathering that makes Thanksgiving, not the food, said Mario. He will always remember his childhood as a time when he was truly hungry. "You serve yourself better when you know where you came from," he said. But at Thanksgiving, he is also reminded that "there is hope. Keep on finding it."

About the recipes: You can never have too many Thanksgiving recipes, so, in addition to dishes served at the home of Carmel and Mario St. Laurent, we took this opportunity to reprint some of Newsday's most enduring holiday recipes.

Acra

MAKES 12 SERVINGS

These Caribbean morsels are delicious, so it's worth the effort to seek out yucca, which is found at Latin markets and some supermarkets.

4 yucca, 1¼ to 2 pounds each
4 eggs
4 teaspoons baking powder
1 tablespoon salt
2 teaspoons white pepper
4 tablespoons flour
¾ cup finely chopped parsley
1 tablespoon hot sauce
Salt and black pepper to taste
2 quarts vegetable oil

1. Peel the yucca and either grate by hand or, using a food processor, first shred and then pulse the yucca until it is finely grated. Mix with all the remaining ingredients except the oil.
2. In a deep fryer or deep pot, heat the oil until it reaches 375 degrees. Drop the yucca mixture by tablespoonfuls in the hot oil, being careful not to crowd the pot. Fry until golden, about 3 minutes. Drain on paper towels and serve warm.

Potage a l'Oignon

MAKES 10 TO 12 SERVINGS

This creamy version of the classic French onion soup is a holiday favorite at the St. Laurent house.

12 cups chicken stock or canned broth
1 cup half-and-half
½ cup (1 stick) butter or margarine
1 cup finely chopped onion
½ cup plus 2 tablespoons flour
1 tablespoon salt
Parmesan croutons (see note)

1. In a large pot, bring the stock and half-and-half to a boil. Set aside.
2. In a saucepan, melt the butter and add the onion and saute until translucent. Add the flour and whisk for about 2 minutes over medium heat.
3. Add the onion mixture to the stock and cook over medium heat until the soup begins to thicken. Strain the soup and discard the onions. Add the salt. Garnish with the croutons and serve immediately.
Note: To make Parmesan croutons, slice french bread into ½-inch-thick slices. Mix ¼ cup unsalted butter with 4 ounces grated Parmesan. Spread on bread and bake in 350-degree oven until golden, 5 to 10 minutes.

Pepper Gravy

MAKES 12 SERVINGS

The Thanksgiving gravy served at the St. Laurent feast is a lively mix of onion and green pepper with a hint of tomato.

3 cups pan drippings or chicken broth (see note)
1 medium onion, thinly sliced
1 medium green pepper, thinly sliced
2 tablespoons tomato paste
1½ tablespoons cornstarch
Salt and pepper to taste

1. In a saucepan, bring all the ingredients except cornstarch and seasoning to a boil. Cover and simmer for 10 minutes, or until vegetables are very soft.
2. Make a slurry by mixing the cornstarch with 3 table-spoons of water. Add to the saucepan and continue to cook the gravy until it thickens, about 2 to 5 minutes more. Season to taste with salt and pepper.
Note: This can be made ahead of time with canned or pre-made broth instead of pan drippings.

Ultimate Recipe for Turkey Gravy

MAKES 12 SERVINGS

This is a traditional Thanksgiving gravy, from Newsday columnist Marie Bianco.

Turkey drippings, or 4 tablespoons butter or margarine
6 tablespoons all-purpose flour
½ teaspoon salt
Freshly ground black pepper
3 cups turkey broth (see note)
1 cup finely chopped cooked giblets (see note)

In a pan, heat the turkey drippings, butter or margarine (if using drippings, make gravy right in roasting pan). Add the flour, salt and pepper. Stir until bubbly. Add the broth slow-ly, stirring constantly, and cook until thickened. Stir in 1 cup chopped cooked giblets. Cook 2 to 3 minutes. Adjust sea-soning.
Note: Make the turkey broth the day before cooking the gravy. Place the turkey neck, heart and gizzard in saucepan. Add 1 chopped onion, 1 chopped carrot, 1 stalk celery, a sprig of parsley, a bay leaf and several peppercorns. Cover with water and cook for 2 hours or until the meat is tender. Add the liver and simmer 5 minutes. Remove from heat and chill quickly. Remove the congealed fat and strain broth. Chop the giblets and neck meat.

How to Roast a Turkey

Even the veteran Thanksgiving cook might roast a whole turkey only once a year and need to have his or her memory refreshed on the basics of buying, thawing and cooking the bird. Here are a few tips, followed by roast-ing instructions.
•Buy at least 1 pound of uncooked turkey for each person if you're serving a whole bird and want leftovers.
•If you buy a frozen bird, you can thaw it in the refrig-erator, in cold water or in the microwave. A whole turkey takes about 24 hours for every 5 pounds to thaw in the refrigerator. In cold water, it takes about 30 minutes for each pound (change the water every 30 minutes). For microwave thawing, follow the manufacturer's instruc-tions for the size turkey that will fit in your oven, the minutes for each pound and the proper power level. (Also worth noting: Turkey thawed in the microwave should be cooked immediately.) Never defrost a turkey on the counter. And once thawed, keep the turkey refrig-erated at 40 degrees or below until ready to cook.
•If you cook your dressing inside the turkey, don't stuff the bird until right before it's placed in the oven to avoid possible contamination by harmful bacteria. Furthermore, if you make the dressing ahead of time, refrigerate the wet and dry ingredients separately, and combine them right before stuffing the turkey. Be sure to stuff the turkey loosely, about ¾ cup stuffing for each pound of turkey.
•Use a two-step test for turkey doneness: Insert a meat thermometer into the deepest portion of the thigh, not touching bone. Once the thigh has reached 180 degrees, move the thermometer to the center of the stuffing. When the stuffing reaches 160 to 165 degrees, the turkey can be removed from the oven.

To roast a turkey, preheat the oven to 325 degrees. Place the bird breast-side up on a rack in a shallow roasting pan. If cooking the stuffing inside the turkey, fill the body cavity with stuffing now. Insert a meat ther-mometer into the thickest part of the thigh, not touching bone (or use an instant-read thermometer later as the turkey roasts). Place the turkey on the lowest oven rack, and roast it uncovered until the meat thermometer regis-ters 180 degrees. Use the roasting timetable (at right) to estimate approximate cooking time. If stuffed, make sure the temperature of the stuffing has reached 160 to 165 degrees before removing the turkey from the oven.

Roasting guidelines for a fresh or thawed turkey

Roast at 325 degrees in a conventional oven on the lowest oven rack

Weight	Unstuffed turkey	Stuffed turkey
8 to 12 pounds	2¾ to 3 hours	3 to 3½ hours
12 to 14 pounds	3 to 3¾ hours	3½ to 4 hours
14 to 18 pounds	3¾ to 4¼ hours	4 to 4½ hours
18 to 20 pounds	4¼ to 4½ hours	4¼ to 5¼ hours
20 to 24 pounds	4½ to 5 hours	4¾ to 5¼ hours

SOURCE: The National Turkey Federation

Cranberry-Orange Sauce

MAKES 8 SERVINGS

This is slightly zingier than the side-of-the-bag cranberry sauce, but if you prefer it mild, simply omit the hot pepper. The recipe is easily doubled to serve 16 – or to provide plenty of leftovers for those who like to tuck some cranberry sauce into their turkey sandwiches.

1 (12-ounce) bag cranberries, fresh or frozen
1 cup sugar
1 cup water
Grated zest of ½ orange
Pinch of crumbled, dried hot pepper flakes

In a saucepan, combine the cranberries, sugar, water, orange zest and pepper flakes. Over high heat, bring to a boil, then turn down to medium heat and stir and cook for about 10 minutes, or until the berries have burst and the sauce is thickened.

National Rice

MAKES 10 TO 12 SERVINGS

No holiday would be complete at the St. Laurent house without this rice dish.

4 tablespoons olive oil
2 tablespoons diced onion
2 tablespoons minced garlic
3 cups chicken broth
1 (15-ounce) can red kidney beans (do not drain)
2 cups converted rice, uncooked
1 teaspoon salt

In a large pot, heat the oil and saute the onions and garlic until golden, about 10 minutes. Add the broth and bring to a boil. Add the beans with their liquid, the rice and salt, and simmer, covered, for 17 minutes or until the liquid is absorbed and the rice is tender.

Garlicked Brussels Sprouts

MAKES 8 SERVINGS

If possible, buy farmstand Brussels sprouts still on the stalk; they keep better. If not, make sure to buy bright green, fresh sprouts, not ones that have turned yellow.

1 (10¾-ounce) can chicken broth
2 stalks or 3 (1-pint) cartons Brussels sprouts
3 tablespoons butter
3 tablespoons olive oil
5 cloves garlic, peeled and finely minced
Zest of 1 lemon
Salt and fresh ground pepper, to taste

1. In a wide saucepan, heat the chicken broth and enough water to make ½ inch of liquid. While bringing the liquid to a simmer, pull any discolored or drying leaves off the sprouts and cut an X in the stem of each sprout. (This is so the sprouts and the leaves cook in the same amount of time.) Rinse in cold water and add to the simmering liquid in a single layer. (Do in batches if necessary.) Cover the pot and cook gently for about 8 minutes, depending on size of the sprouts, or until still slightly crunchy in the center. Remove the sprouts with a slotted spoon, reserving the broth. Return the broth to high heat and boil until the liquid is reduced to about ¼ cup.

2. Heat the butter and olive oil in a wide skillet. Add the garlic and saute until it begins to brown. Add the sprouts to the skillet, toss to coat well. Then add the reduced broth, sprinkle with lemon zest and add salt and pepper to taste. Toss and cook a few more minutes. (You may need to do this in 2 batches, too, if the skillet is not big enough to hold all the sprouts without crowding.)

Carmel St. Laurent with a bountiful plate of Thanksgiving favorites

Yams With Apricot Orange Sauce

MAKES 6 SERVINGS

This recipe satisfies those who crave sweet yams, without the addition of marsh-mallows. The garnet sweet potatoes found at times in supermarkets can be used instead of yams. The recipe may be doubled to make 12 servings.

⅓ cup light brown sugar, packed
4 teaspoons cornstarch
¼ teaspoon cinnamon
Dash salt
1 cup Sauternes wine
½ cup orange juice
1 tablespoon butter
1 cup dried apricots (if large, chopped)
¼ cup raisins, preferably golden
6 medium yams, cooked and sliced, or 3 (1-pound)
    cans yams, drained and sliced

1. Mix in a saucepan the brown sugar, cornstarch, cinnamon and salt. Gradually stir in the wine and orange juice. Place over medium heat and stir constantly until the sauce boils and let it boil about 30 seconds. Add the butter, apricots and raisins. Stir until the butter melts.
2. Transfer the yams to a casserole and pour the sauce over them. Bake at 350 degrees for 10 minutes to heat through. Alternatively, prepare the casserole a day ahead and refrigerate, let sit at room temperature for an hour and bake about 30 minutes or until heated through, or reheat in a microwave.

Potato Stuffing

MAKES 10 TO 12 SERVINGS

This savory stuffing can be baked in the oven or inside the turkey. The sisters sometimes use sausage instead of the beef, or corn in place of the peas.

1 pound ground beef
2 ribs celery, chopped
1 medium onion, chopped
2 medium carrots, diced
1 cup peas, frozen or canned
1 tablespoon chopped garlic
5 baking potatoes (about 3½ pounds), peeled and cubed
3 eggs
1 tablespoon salt
1 teaspoon black pepper
1 teaspoon poultry seasoning

1. In a large saute pan, combine the beef, celery, onion, carrots, peas and garlic. Brown the mixture over medium-high heat, breaking up the meat with a wooden spoon, until the meat is cooked through.
2. In a large pot, cover the potatoes with water and bring to a boil. Simmer for 10 minutes. Drain and set aside. If cooking the stuffing outside the bird, preheat the oven to 350 degrees.
3. In a large bowl, beat the eggs. Add the salt, pepper and poultry seasoning. Add the beef and vegetables and the potatoes and combine thoroughly.
4. Place the stuffing into a greased 9-by-13-inch baking dish and bake for 30 minutes, or use to stuff a turkey. Makes enough to stuff a 20-pound turkey.

Corn Bread Dressing

MAKES MORE THAN 12 SERVINGS

Southerners and Midwesterners say dressing, not stuffing, and it is usually cooked outside the bird. Here is a traditional recipe.

½ cup (1 stick) butter
1 large shallot, minced
1½ cups minced onion
1½ cups minced celery
2 teaspoons crumbled marjoram
1 tablespoon crumbled dried sage
2 teaspoons dried thyme
½ teaspoon celery seed
7 eggs
8 thick slices white bread, stale or dry
10 cups crumbled corn bread (recipe follows)
1 (32-ounce) package chicken broth, or
   turkey or chicken stock
2 teaspoons salt
1 teaspoon black pepper

1. Melt the butter in a large skillet and add the shallot, onion and celery. Saute, stirring occasionally, until the vegetables are limp and translucent. While cooking, add marjoram, sage, thyme and celery seed.

2. In a very large bowl, beat eggs lightly. Crumble the bread and corn bread into fine crumbs and add. Add the contents of the skillet, broth, salt and pepper. If the mixture is not moist enough, add up to 1 cup of water. It should be soft but not soupy. Transfer to a greased 9-by-13-inch baking dish and bake at 375 degrees for 1 hour or until browned on top.

Corn Bread for Dressing

For a traditional Southern dressing, use unsweetened corn bread.

2 tablespoons bacon fat or vegetable oil
6 cups cornmeal, white or yellow, or part each
1 tablespoon baking soda
2 teaspoons salt
2 eggs, lightly beaten
6 cups buttermilk

1. Preheat the oven to 450 degrees. While the oven is preheating, place 1 tablespoon of bacon fat or oil in each of 2 (10-inch) black-iron skillets or other heavy, ovenproof skillets and set in the oven to heat.

2. In a large bowl, combine the cornmeal, baking soda and salt. Fluff with a fork to mix together. Add the eggs and buttermilk and stir to combine. When the skillets of fat are smoking hot, carefully remove one from the oven, pour the fat into the batter and stir in quickly, then pour the batter into the skillet and return to the oven. Repeat. (If you have only 1 skillet, do this in 2 batches.) Bake for 25 minutes or until golden brown. Makes 2 large corn breads, or enough for the corn bread dressing recipe.

Creamy onion soup is enjoyed at the children's table, above left. Dr. Mario St. Laurent and guests sit down to Thanksgiving dinner, above.

Sweet Potato Pudding

MAKES 10 TO 12 SERVINGS

Carmel St. Laurent's sweet potato bread is made with a tropical sweet potato, which is white inside and can be found in Latin markets. We adapted her recipe using common sweet potatoes to make a pudding.

6 cups grated sweet potatoes
3 sliced ripe bananas
1 cup sweetened coconut milk
4 cups half-and-half
9 eggs, lightly beaten
1½ cups sugar
1 cup raisins
1 teaspoon ground cinnamon
1 teaspoon nutmeg
2 tablespoons vanilla extract

Preheat the oven to 350 degrees. Mix all the ingredients and place in 2 (9-by-13-inch) baking dishes. Bake for 1½ hours, or until the pudding is set and browned on top.

Pecan Pie

MAKES 8 SERVINGS

This recipe is from a tearoom in New Orleans. It couldn't be simpler.

4 eggs
¼ teaspoon salt
4 tablespoons butter, melted
1¼ cups light corn syrup
1¼ cups packed brown sugar
1 teaspoon vanilla extract
1 unbaked 9-inch piecrust
1 cup chopped pecans

Preheat the oven to 350 degrees. Beat the eggs with a whisk. Add the salt, butter, corn syrup, brown sugar and vanilla and mix well. Pour into the piecrust. Sprinkle with the pecans. Bake for 45 to 50 minutes. Transfer to a rack. The filling will set as the pie cools.

The Perfect Piecrust

Some piecrust recipes call for vinegar, cream cheese, hot water and other "secret" ingredients. Fear not. Using only flour, shortening, salt and water, these are the only tips you need to make perfect piecrust:
• Forget about measuring the water exactly. In humid weather, flour may be more moist, and at other times it will be dryer. Use just enough ice cold water to make the dough come together in a ball.
• Do not work the dough too much, as this toughens it. (Adding too little water can cause you to overwork the dough.)
• Chill the crust before rolling, if possible, and again up until you bake it.

This recipe makes enough for 2 or 3 single-crust pies, depending on size, or 1 double crust pie.

　2½ cups all-purpose flour, or a combination of 2 cups
　　all-purpose and ½ cup low-protein flour such as
　　White Lily or ½ cup cake flour (not self-rising)
　½ teaspoon salt
　1 cup (2 sticks) cold, unsalted butter, cut into small
　　pieces, or ¾ cup lard or vegetable shortening
　Ice water
1. Place flour and salt in bowl and fluff with a fork to mix. Using clean fingertips or a pastry blender, cut butter, lard or vegetable shortening into the flour. The mix-ture should resemble coarse crumbs.
2. Put ice cubes in a 1-cup measuring cup and fill it with water. Pour about 3 or 4 tablespoons water into the bowl, and using a fork, blend into flour quickly. Add enough additional water to make the dough come together in a ball. Do not mix more. Wrap dough in waxed paper or enclose in a sealable plastic bag, and refrigerate for at least 30 minutes.
3. For single crust pies that are to be filled later, pre-heat oven to 375 degrees.
4. Break off half the dough and, using a floured rolling pin, roll out evenly on a lightly floured board, using quick, sure strokes and working from the center. Roll dough an inch or so larger than the pie plate, so that you have plenty to work with. Fold into quarters and place with the point in the center of the pie plate. Unfold to fit plate. Trim and crimp edges.
5. Lay a piece of waxed paper, foil or parchment paper in the piecrust and fill completely with weights such as raw rice or beans. Bake 20 minutes in the center of the preheated oven. Remove weights and paper or foil and cover edges of pie with foil if browning too fast. Bake about 5 more minutes.
6. Alternatively, when baking a pie and a filling at the same time, follow recipe instructions, but while preheat-ing oven, preheat a cookie sheet. Slide pie directly onto cookie sheet to bake, which will help make a crisp crust.

Pumpkin Pie With Ginger Streusel

MAKES 8 SERVINGS

This ginger streusel-topped pumpkin pie is richer than the usual pumpkin pie. An entire stick of butter is used to bind the nuts, brown sugar and crystallized ginger for the topping. The filling is laden with cream and eggs. It's great the next day, too — if it lasts that long.

For the filling:
1 (16-ounce) can solid pack pumpkin
1½ cups heavy cream
3 large eggs
½ cup sugar
¼ cup packed light brown sugar
2¼ teaspoons pumpkin pie spice
¼ teaspoon salt
1 (9-inch) deep-dish piecrust, baked
For the topping:
1 cup flour
½ cup packed light brown sugar
½ cup coarsely chopped walnuts
⅓ cup finely chopped crystallized ginger
1½ teaspoons ground ginger
½ cup (1 stick) unsalted butter, cut
    into small pieces, at room temperature

1. Preheat the oven to 350 degrees.
2. To make the filling, whisk all the ingredients in a large bowl until combined. Pour into the piecrust. Bake until a skin begins to form on the filling and the filling begins to set, about 50 minutes. Remove from oven. Let pie stand 10 minutes to set slightly. Maintain oven temperature.
3. Meanwhile, prepare the topping. Mix the flour, light brown sugar, walnuts, crystallized ginger and ground ginger in a medium bowl. Blend in the butter with your fingertips until the mixture begins to form small clumps.
4. Sprinkle the topping over the pie. Bake until the pie is set and the streusel is golden brown, about 25 minutes. Transfer to a rack and cool completely.

The combined St. Laurent-Joseph-Jean-Adrian family and friends gather for the carving of the turkey.

C H A P T E R I I

HOLIDAY COOKIE PARTY

Menu

Chocolate Fudge Cookies
Peanut Blossoms
Raspberry Squares
Kourabiedes (Greek Sugar Cookies)
Chocolate Chip Nut Rolls
Lemon Crescents
Sand Tarts
Bourbon Balls
Pecan Tarts
Fabulous Fudge
Cookie Press Butter Cookies
Seven-Layer Cookies
Roz' Chocolate Chip Cookies

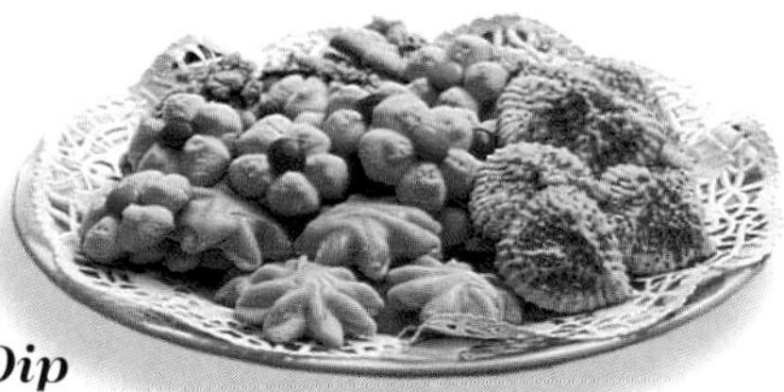

Maria Lynn's Cookie Party Artichoke Dip
Hot Mulled Cider

A group of teachers gets into

the holiday spirit by swapping

confections and recipes

A SWEET AFFAIR

Beginning in late November and continuing into early December, bakers all over Long Island gather for an event that heralds the season, the holiday cookie party, where they share old family recipes, swap goodies and spread cheer. Each of the parties operates a little differently, and the annual gathering at the Lloyd Neck home of Maria Lynn has been going on long enough that it has its own traditions. For one, the party, attended mostly by Maria's fellow teachers at Stimson Middle School in Huntington Station, is always held on a Friday afternoon so the guests can come straight from work and unwind. Mulled cider is always in plentiful supply. And it's never long after the guests arrive that they start asking Maria when her hot artichoke dip will be ready, lest they start devouring the main attractions displayed in their holiday finery on the dining room table.

More than 1,000 cookies — powdered, iced, rolled, molded, pressed, layered, nut-crusted and rum-soaked

Maria Lynn's daughter-in-law, Mary Coleman, and grandson, Connor, admire the Christmas tree.

— are exchanged at Maria's party. It works like this: Each guest is asked to bring four dozen cookies and the recipe. At the end of the party, each guest selects four dozen cookies — a few of each kind — to take home, and copies of the recipes are compiled into booklets. "There isn't enough to give away as gifts," said Maria of each guest's haul. "That's not what this is for. But you do get enough to serve at a holiday gathering. It's a beautiful assortment."

Maria tries to encourage her baker and non-baker friends to attend, so, unlike some other cookie party hostesses, she doesn't impose any rules on the kinds of cookies that her guests bring. Maria's sister, Phyllis Freund of Ronkonkoma, knows of a cookie exchange where chocolate chip cookies are banned and the hostess approves all the recipes beforehand. Maria doesn't even insist that her guests bake. Store-bought cookies are graciously accepted at her gathering. "One year one of the teachers had a lot going on in her life, so she just went to Cardinali's in Syosset and got some pirouettes from the bakery," said Maria. "They were a nice addition to the table."

Guests enjoy mulled cider, wine and appetizers before the cookie exchange.

Artichoke Dip

This dip is as eagerly anticipated as the cookies at Maria's annual gathering.

Maria Lynn's Cookie Party Artichoke Dip

1 (14-ounce) can artichoke hearts, finely chopped
1 cup mayonnaise
1 cup grated Parmesan cheese
1 cup shredded mozzarella cheese
2 teaspoons hot sauce
½ teaspoon salt

Preheat the oven to 350 degrees. Combine all the ingredients and mix thoroughly. Place the mixture in a 1½-quart ovenproof dish and bake 30 minutes. Serve warm with crackers. Makes about 3 cups.

Chocolate Fudge Cookies

MAKES 5½ DOZEN

Maria Lynn has been making these dense, moist chocolate cookies for years. The recipe is from the Junior League of Long Island.

1 (12-ounce) package semisweet chocolate chips
4 tablespoons (½ stick) butter
1 (14-ounce) can sweetened condensed milk
1 teaspoon vanilla extract
1 cup flour
1 cup pecans, toasted, cooled and broken into large pieces

1. Preheat the oven to 350 degrees. Line a cookie sheet with aluminum foil, shiny side up.
2. Place the chocolate chips and butter in the top of a large double boiler over warm water on moderate heat (or melt in a microwave oven). Stir until melted and smooth. Remove the mixture from the heat and stir in the condensed milk and vanilla, then the flour, followed by the cooled pecans.
3. Using a rounded teaspoon of mixture for each cookie, place dough 1 to 2 inches apart on the foil. Bake exactly 8 minutes. The cookies will feel very soft but will firm as they cool. When cool, use a spatula to transfer them to a rack.

Peanut Blossoms

MAKES 5 DOZEN

Tracy Cortese of Rockville Centre baked these old fashioned favorites.

1¾ cups all-purpose flour
½ cup sugar, plus additional to roll cookies in
½ cup firmly packed brown sugar
1 teaspoon baking soda
¼ teaspoon salt
½ cup shortening
½ cup peanut butter
2 tablespoons milk
1 teaspoon vanilla extract
1 egg
60 milk chocolate candy kisses, unwrapped

1. Preheat the oven to 375 degrees.
2. In a large bowl, combine the flour, ½ cup sugar, brown sugar, baking soda, salt, shortening, peanut butter, milk, vanilla and egg. Mix at low speed until the dough is stiff.
3. Shape the dough into 1-inch balls, then roll in sugar. Place 2 inches apart on ungreased cookie sheet. Bake for 10 to 12 minutes, or until golden brown. Immediately top each cookie with a candy kiss, pressing down firmly so the cookie cracks around its edges. Remove from the cookie sheet to cool.

Raspberry Squares

MAKES 32 PIECES

Maria Lynn sometimes substitutes apricot jam for the seedless raspberry jam in this recipe.

3 cups flour
¾ cup sugar
3 egg yolks
1 cup (2 sticks) unsalted butter, melted
1 lemon rind, grated
1 (12-ounce) jar seedless raspberry jam

1. Preheat the oven to 350 degrees. Butter a 9-by-13-inch baking dish and set aside.
2. Mix together the flour, sugar, egg yolks, melted butter and lemon rind. Pat ¾ of the dough into the pan and slightly up its sides. Spread with the jam. Sprinkle the rest of the dough on top for crumbs. Bake 45 minutes. Cut into squares when cool.

Kourabiedes (Greek Sugar Cookies)

MAKES 7 DOZEN

Eva Khatana's recipe for these hand-shaped cookies is an old family treasure. The cookies melt in your mouth. Eva, from Bayside, Queens, said Greek bakeries often make them with almonds inside.

1 cup (2 sticks) unsalted butter
⅓ cup confectioners' sugar, plus additional to dust cookies
1 egg yolk
2½ tablespoons brandy or whiskey
¼ teaspoon fresh lemon juice
3 cups sifted flour
¼ teaspoon salt

1. Preheat the oven to 350 degrees.
2. With an electric mixer, cream the butter for 15 minutes. Add ⅓ cup sugar and continue to beat for 2 more minutes. Add the egg yolk and continue to beat for another 2 minutes. Add the brandy or whiskey and lemon juice, and beat 2 more minutes.
3. Add the sifted flour and salt, and mix until the dough is smooth and holds together. Pinch off the dough by the teaspoon and roll into a cigar shape, then bend into a crescent. Place the crescents on a cookie sheet and bake for 15 to 20 minutes. The cookies should be baked through but not browned.
4. Sift a light layer of confectioners' sugar onto a piece of wax paper. Place the warm cookies on top; sift more sugar over them. Let the cookies sit for 20 minutes. Serve in colored mini-muffin paper cups.

Chocolate Chip Nut Rolls

MAKES 4½ DOZEN

Kristin Bernard of Smithtown got this recipe from her mother-in-law. "It's my favorite cookie that she makes, and she makes dozens and dozens of cookies," said Kristin. It's also easy and foolproof.

For the dough:
2¼ cups sifted flour
½ teaspoon salt
¾ cup (1½ sticks) margarine, softened
¾ cup sugar
l egg
1½ teaspoons vanilla extract
1 (6-ounce) package semisweet miniature chocolate chips
For the chocolate coating:
1 (12-ounce) package semisweet chocolate chips
¼ cup margarine
2 cups chopped walnuts

1. Preheat the oven to 350 degrees.
2. Sift together the flour and salt.
3. Beat together the margarine, sugar, egg and vanilla in a large bowl until well mixed. Blend in the flour and salt. Stir in the miniature chocolate chips.
4. On a lightly floured surface, shape the dough into 2-by-½-inch logs. Place on ungreased cookie sheet. Bake for 12 to 15 minutes, or until the cookies are set. Transfer to wire racks to cool.
5. To make the coating, melt the chocolate chips and margarine in the top of double boiler over hot water; stir until blended and smooth. If too thick, add more margarine 1 tablespoon at a time, until it reaches the proper consistency for coating.
6. Dip the ends of the cooled cookies into the chocolate coating, then roll the ends in the chopped walnuts. Place on wax paper until set.

Mulled Cider

Hot mulled cider is a great addition to a holiday party for two reasons: It frees up the hostess while guests help themselves to drinks and it makes the house smell wonderful. Guests can fetch their drinks from the pot on the stove, or, if you have one, a slow-cooker turned to low heat. For those who like their cider "spiked," offer rum on the side.

In a large pot, combine 1 gallon of apple cider, 10 whole cloves, 5 cinnamon sticks, a generous grating of fresh nutmeg and 5 thin slices of lemon. Bring to a boil. Turn heat down and simmer, uncovered, for 15 minutes. Makes 16 to 20 servings.

Lemon Crescents

MAKES 9 DOZEN

Linda Stauder of East Meadow found this recipe in the box of family favorites her mother gave her as a wedding gift 10 years ago. Linda remembers her grandmother making these cookies.

1 cup (2 sticks) butter
1 cup confectioners' sugar, divided
1 teaspoon grated lemon rind
2 cups sifted flour
2 cups finely chopped walnuts

1. In a bowl, mix the butter with ⅓ cup sugar until smooth. Stir in the lemon rind and flour until well-blended. Stir in the walnuts. Chill the dough several hours or overnight.
2. Preheat the oven to 325 degrees.
3. Pinch off the dough a scant teaspoon at a time and roll into 2-inch-long logs between your palms. Place them 1 inch apart on an ungreased cookie sheet. Once on the cookie sheet, curve each log into a crescent.
4. Bake 15 minutes or until firm and delicately golden. Remove immediately from the cookie sheets, and while still hot, roll the cookies in the remaining confectioners' sugar. Place them on a rack to cool. After the cookies have cooled completely, roll them again in the confectioners' sugar.

Sand Tarts

MAKES ABOUT 3½ DOZEN

Barbara Arnold of Port Washington brought these sand tarts to share.

1 cup pecans
½ cup sugar
½ cup (1 stick) butter
½ cup shortening
2 teaspoons vanilla extract
2½ cups flour
Confectioners' sugar for rolling

1. Preheat the oven to 325 degrees. Toast the pecans on a foil-lined cookie sheet for 8 minutes, stirring occasionally. Remove from the oven and set aside to cool.
2. Place the cooled pecans and sugar in a food processor and pulse just enough to finely chop the pecans.
3. In a large mixing bowl, cream the butter and shortening. Add the vanilla. Mix in the pecan and sugar mixture and stir until smooth. Gradually add the flour.
4. Shape into 1-inch balls and place on a parchment-lined cookie sheet and bake for 20 minutes or until the bottoms begin to brown. When cooled, roll in confectioners' sugar.

Bourbon Balls

MAKES 4 DOZEN

Fran Lundstrom of Huntington calls these "turkey balls" because she uses 100-proof Wild Turkey bourbon when she makes them.

1 cup vanilla wafer cookie crumbs
1 cup finely chopped pecans
1 cup sifted confectioners' sugar
1 tablespoon cocoa powder
¼ cup bourbon
1½ teaspoons light corn syrup
Confectioners' sugar for rolling

Combine the cookie crumbs, pecans, sugar and cocoa. Blend the bourbon and corn syrup, then add to the dry ingredients and mix well. Form the dough into 1-inch balls, then roll them in confectioners' sugar. Chill until firm.

Pecan Tarts

MAKES 2 DOZEN

This is from Susan Conlin, of Huntington, who got it from a friend.

For the dough:
1 (3-ounce) package cream cheese
½ cup (1 stick) butter
1 cup flour
For the filling:
¾ cup pecans
½ cup brown sugar
1 egg
1 tablespoon softened butter
1 teaspoon vanilla extract

1. Preheat the oven to 350 degrees.
2. Toast the pecans on foil-lined cookie sheet for 8 minutes. Set aside to cool.
3. In a mixing bowl, blend the cream cheese and butter. Add the flour and mix until the dough holds together.
4. Line a mini-muffin tin with shortening or nonstick cooking spray. Pinch off 2 teaspoons of dough at a time and roll into a ball, flatten the ball slightly and shape into a mini-muffin cup, pressing the dough up along the sides of the cup. Proceed this way for all 24 cups, or until all the dough is used up.
5. To prepare the filling, place the pecans and brown sugar in a food processor and chop until nuts are finely cut but not pasty. In a small mixing bowl, beat the egg, then add the softened butter and vanilla. Add the brown sugar and pecan mixture and blend until smooth.
6. Fill each dough-lined cup with 1 teaspoon of filling, being careful not to overfill. The cup should be ⅞ths full to allow for expansion when baking. There may be a tablespoon of filling leftover, but resist the temptation to go back and add filling to the cups.
7. Bake for 30 minutes in a 350-degree oven or until the crust is slightly brown. When they are cool enough to handle, remove each pecan tart from its cup, using a sharp paring knife to loosen the edges if necessary.

Fabulous Fudge

MAKES 48 PIECES

This recipe is from Karen Teufel of West Babylon. It's easy enough that everyone in her family, non-cooks included, can make it.

¾ cup evaporated milk or light cream
1 tablespoon butter or margarine
1½ cups sugar
16 marshmallows, cut in half, or 1 (10-ounce) bag miniature marshmallows
1 (12-ounce) package semisweet chocolate chips
1 cup chopped nuts
1 teaspoon vanilla extract

1. Combine the milk, butter, sugar and marshmallows in a 2-quart, microwave-safe bowl. Microwave on high for 3 to 4 minutes, or until the marshmallows puff and the mixture begins to boil. Stir it well. Microwave the mixture for 2 more minutes, then stir again. Microwave again for 1 minute or until the mixture boils and the sugar is completely dissolved.
2. Stir in the chocolate chips, nuts and vanilla extract. Beat until the chocolate chips have melted and the mixture is well-blended. Spread in an 8-by-8-inch buttered baking dish. Let cool, then refrigerate for 1 hour. Cut into small squares.

Cookie Press Butter Cookies

MAKES 6 TO 7 DOZEN

This recipe comes from Phyllis Freund of Ronkonkoma, Maria Lynn's sister.

2 cups (4 sticks) unsalted butter, softened
1 cup plus 2 tablespoons sugar
2 eggs
1 teaspoon vanilla extract
l teaspoon salt
4 cups flour

1. Preheat the oven to 375 degrees.
2. Mix together the butter, sugar, eggs, vanilla and salt. Work in the flour until blended. The dough will be stiff. Fill a cookie press with ¼ of the dough and select a disc. Press cookies onto an ungreased baking sheet. Bake 9 to 12 minutes until the cookies are set but not brown; do not overbake.

Seven-Layer Cookies

MAKES 4 DOZEN

This is an adaptation of a recipe from Christine Di Lorenzo, who lives in Huntington.

½ cup (1 stick) margarine
1 cup graham cracker crumbs
1 cup semisweet chocolate chips
1 cup butterscotch or peanut butter chips
¾ cup shredded sweetened coconut
1 (14-ounce) can sweetened condensed milk
½ cup chopped walnuts

1. Preheat the oven to 350 degrees.
2. In a saucepan, melt the margarine. Add the graham cracker crumbs and stir until the crumbs are moist. Press the mixture into the bottom of a 9-by-13-inch pan, and bake for 5 minutes.
3. Sprinkle the chocolate chips and butterscotch or peanut butter chips evenly over the baked crumbs. Top with the coconut. Drizzle the can of sweetened condensed milk evenly over the top. Sprinkle with the walnuts.
4. Bake for 25 minutes. Allow to cool for 30 minutes and cut into small squares before completely cooled. Let the cookies finish cooling fully before removing them from the pan.

Opposite, clockwise from bottom left, kourabiedes, peanut blossoms, fabulous fudge, cookie press butter cookies and raspberry squares

At right, host Maria Lynn

Butter vs. Shortening in Baking

When Gerry Morgan of Hauppauge brought this recipe to Maria Lynn's cookie exchange, she insisted that it be made with shortening, not butter. "My mother always made it with Crisco," she said. "It makes a difference."

Does it? At Newsday, we decided to test whether there is a difference between using butter or shortening in cookies. The difference between our two batches of cookies was dramatic.

The dough made with vegetable shortening was more crumbly and felt drier than the one made with butter. The shortening cookie rose more and was lighter and airier than the butter cookie, which was flat, crisp and crunchy. As for taste, our testers were evenly divided.

Cooks have a choice of fats when baking, said Shirley Corriher, food scientist and cookbook author, and they should choose depending on what type of cookie is desired.

Butter melts at a lower temperature, so it spreads faster than vegetable shortening. But because butter is about 20 percent water, shortening is richer in fat. Corriher said if you're going to substitute shortening in a recipe calling for butter, use 20 percent less shortening. If you're going to substitute butter in a recipe calling for shortening, use 20 percent more butter. Her compromise: Use butter-flavored shortening.

Gerry Morgan named these favorites after her mother, who always used Crisco.

Roz' Chocolate Chip Cookies
2¼ cups flour
1 teaspoon baking soda
½ teaspoon salt
1 cup vegetable shortening
½ cup granulated sugar
¾ cup dark brown sugar, packed
1 teaspoon vanilla extract
2 eggs
1 (12-ounce) package semisweet chocolate chips

1. Preheat the oven to 375 degrees.
2. Combine flour, baking soda and salt in a small bowl. Beat vegetable shortening, sugars and vanilla in a large mixing bowl. Add the eggs, 1 at a time, beating well after each. Gradually beat in the flour mixture. Stir in the chocolate chips. Drop by rounded teaspoonful onto ungreased baking sheets.
3. Bake for 9 to 11 minutes or until golden brown. Let the cookies stand for 2 minutes, then remove to wire racks to cool completely. Makes 5 dozen.

The exchange: Guests make their selections from the hundreds of cookies.

CHANUKAH

Menu

Israeli Chopped Salad
Hummus
Tabbouleh
Eggplant Salad
Stuffed Potato Patties
Meat Latkes
Potato Latkes
Applesauce

Kahee
Soufganioth

An Israeli-Iraqi family

celebrates the miracle of the oil

with a kid-friendly gathering

THE FESTIVAL OF LIGHTS

T he lighting of one candle on each of the eight nights of Chanukah commemorates the holiday's central miracle: After the Maccabees, a family of Jewish insurgents, led a successful revolt against their Greek oppressors in 165 B.C., the battle-ravaged temple in Jerusalem had only enough oil on hand to keep the eternal light kindled for one day. Miraculously, the oil lasted for eight days, by which time more oil had arrived.

The whole Chanukah story revolves around this precious oil, and now the holiday is doubly beloved as a celebration of political liberation and of fried foods. At the Dix Hills home of Lily and Eric Engelhardt, the Festival of Lights is done up big. At their annual party, menorahs of all description are everywhere as are bags of Chanukah gelt and small wooden dreidels. There are Chanukah platters, Chanukah cookie jars, Chanukah napkin holders, Chanukah salt and pepper shakers.

When guests arrive, many of the dishes have already been set out on the buffet table, including tabbouleh, chopped Israeli salad and hummus. But the fried foods,

From left in foreground, Andrew Schwartz, Dana Schwartz and Natalie Engelhardt light the menorahs.

such as the latkes and stuffed patties, have to be done at the last minute. That job falls to Lily and her mother, Matilda Korine, who was born and raised in Iraq, but whose family moved to Israel in the '50s. The entire clan, led by Lily, moved from Israel to Long Island in the '80s. Now Lily's family, her parents and her two siblings and their families live, almost kibbutz-style, within five minutes of one another.

Once the sun sets, the children congregate to partake in the most important moments of any Chanukah celebration — the lighting of the candles. Then it's time for dessert. Alongside the *soufganioth*, fried doughnuts, is a pile of *kahee*, fried disks of puff pastry. It doesn't escape Matilda that soufganioth (a flour-egg-margarine batter fried in hot oil and sprinkled with sugar) and kahee (a flour-margarine-sugar dough fried in hot oil and sprinkled with sugar) aren't all that dissimilar. But she recalls a time back in the old country, before the nice houses in Dix Hills, when a family might not have much in the larder if a festive dessert was called for. Striking an ecumenical note, Matilda quotes Mohammed, whose family also hailed from the arid sands of the Levant: "The prophet Mohammed said, 'If you have in the house flour, sugar and oil, you have all you need to make guests happy.'"

Above right, Lily Engelhardt serves a plate of food. With her is her husband, Eric, and their children.

Natalie Engelhardt, Dana Schwartz, and Perri and Robyn Korine take turns spinning the dreidel.

Israeli Chopped Salad

MAKES 12 SERVINGS

Lily Engelhardt abhors a chopped salad in which the ingredients are cut too big. She insists on a precise ¼-inch dice for her version.

5 large tomatoes
5 kirby cucumbers, peeled
1 large red pepper
1 large green pepper
3 to 4 scallions
5 to 6 radishes
2 tablespoons finely chopped fresh dill
Juice of 1 lemon
2 tablespoons olive oil
Salt and pepper to taste

Cut all the vegetables into ¼-inch dice. Combine the diced vegetables with the dill, lemon juice, olive oil, salt and pepper. Serve immediately.

Hummus

MAKES 12 SERVINGS

The traditional Israeli presentation of hummus is to put it in a shallow bowl, swirl the surface with a circular motion using the back of a spoon and drizzle olive oil into the middle. Sprinkle with paprika and garnish with black olives and parsley.

3 (15-ounce) cans chick-peas, drained
2 cloves garlic
6 tablespoons lemon juice
6 tablespoons tahini (sesame paste)
¾ cup water
Salt and pepper to taste
Extra-virgin olive oil
Paprika
Parsley, chopped
Black olives

Combine the chick-peas, garlic, lemon juice, tahini, water and salt and pepper to taste in a blender or the bowl of a food processor and process until smooth. Depending on the capacity of your machine, you may have to prepare this in batches. Place the hummus in a serving bowl and drizzle with olive oil. Top with a dash of paprika and the chopped parsley and garnish with the black olives.

Tabbouleh

MAKES 12 SERVINGS

Lily Engelhardt likes to make her tabbouleh with as much mint as parsley, but you can vary the proportions according to your taste. Most supermarkets carry boxed tabbouleh mixes, but loose bulgur can be purchased in Middle Eastern grocery stores and gourmet shops.

1 cup fine bulgur
½ cup finely chopped scallions
1 cup finely chopped parsley
1 cup finely chopped mint
½ cup olive oil
⅓ cup lemon juice
Salt and pepper to taste
3 tomatoes, diced

Soak the bulgur in cold water for 20 minutes, then drain it in a colander until dry. Place in a large bowl and stir in the scallions, parsley and mint. Add the oil, lemon juice and salt and pepper to taste. Right before serving, stir in the diced tomatoes.

Eggplant Salad

MAKES 12 SERVINGS

Roasting the eggplant gives this salad a smoky flavor.

3 eggplants
2 to 4 cloves garlic
¼ cup tahini (sesame paste)
Juice of 2 lemons
Salt to taste
2 tablespoons finely chopped parsley

1. Preheat the oven to 350 degrees. Pierce the eggplants with a fork and bake on a cookie sheet until they are soft inside and their skins are charred, 20 to 30 minutes. Remove from the oven and let cool on a rack.
2. When the eggplants can be handled, peel them and squeeze out any extra juice. In a blender or the bowl of a food processor, combine the eggplants with the garlic, tahini, lemon juice and salt and puree until smooth. Chill and serve garnished with chopped parsley.

From left, Arieh, Avi, Gil and Shula Korine at the Chanukah buffet.

Stuffed Potato Patties

MAKES 30 PATTIES

These stuffed patties — a sort of deluxe version of latkes — are a bit of work, but well worth it. And they can be formed ahead of time and then frozen.

For the potato crust:
3 pounds potatoes, peeled and cut into 2-inch chunks
4 eggs
6 tablespoons flour
Salt and pepper to taste
For the filling:
4 tablespoons vegetable oil
1 pound onions, finely chopped
½ teaspoon salt
½ teaspoon pepper
1 pound ground beef, lamb or turkey
2 ribs celery, finely chopped
¼ cup raisins
¼ cup slivered almonds or pine nuts
2 teaspoons baharat (see recipe)
¼ teaspoon ground cardamom
Vegetable oil for frying
1½ cups bread crumbs

1. Boil the potatoes until soft, then mash until smooth. Set aside, and when cool, stir in the eggs, flour, salt and pepper to make a soft dough.
2. To make the filling, heat the 4 tablespoons oil in a skillet. Add the onions, salt and pepper and saute until the onions are translucent. Add the ground meat, breaking it up with a fork, and cook until it loses its pinkness. Add the celery, raisins, nuts, baharat and cardamom and cook for 5 minutes more. Set the mixture aside to cool.
3. With wet hands, roll 2 tablespoons of the potato mixture into a 2-inch ball. (If the mixture is too loose to handle, add more flour a teaspoon at a time.) Flatten the ball into a patty, place a rounded tablespoonful of the filling in the center, and close up the patty around the filling, reforming it into a ball. Then flatten it into a patty. Repeat until all the dough and filling are used. (At this point, patties can be refrigerated for 2 days or frozen. Defrost them and/or bring them to room temperature before proceeding with recipe.)
4. In a large skillet, heat ¼ inch of oil over medium-high heat. Dredge the patties in the bread crumbs and fry in batches until golden brown, 4 or 5 minutes on each side. Replenish the oil as needed, making sure it's hot before proceeding. Drain the patties on paper towels and serve immediately.

**Matilda Korine, Lily Engelhardt's
mother, prepares stuffed potato patties.**

Baharat

One thing that distinguishes Lily Engelhardt's stuffed potato patties from your average croquette is baharat, a Mediterranean spice mixture that lends an exotic undertone to any savory dish. In fact, baharat is Arabic for spice mixture and, according to Mediterranean food scholar Clifford A. Wright, every Middle Eastern cuisine has a version of it. While virtually all baharats will contain peppercorns, allspice, cinnamon and nutmeg, the variations are almost infinite.

Baharat is available at Middle Eastern markets. Or, you can easily make your own. Use the following recipe as a guide. The dominant ingredients should be peppercorns and allspice berries, but the remaining spices can be augmented with (or replaced by) paprika, sumac or cardamom seeds.

Baharat

¼ cup black peppercorns
¼ cup allspice berries
1 teaspoon coriander seeds
1 teaspoon cumin seeds
2 teaspoons ground cinnamon
1 teaspoon freshly grated nutmeg

Grind the peppercorns, allspice, coriander and cumin seeds together and blend with the cinnamon and nutmeg. Store in a jar in your spice rack, away from sunlight. The mixture will lose pungency as time goes by, but properly stored it can remain good for many months. Makes about ½ cup.

Meat Latkes

MAKES 36 LATKES

Using a nonstick pan reduces the amount of oil you'll need to fry these latkes. To make these even more healthful, Lily Engelhardt usually uses turkey meat.

2 pounds ground beef or turkey
4 large potatoes, peeled and grated
  on medium holes of a box grater
4 large onions, finely chopped
1 bunch parsley, chopped
6 eggs
Salt and pepper to taste
1 teaspoon ground cumin
Vegetable oil for frying

1. Thoroughly combine all the ingredients except the oil. Film the bottom of a large skillet with oil and place it over medium-high heat.
2. Working in batches, drop heaping tablespoonfuls of the mixture into the pan and flatten them slightly. Fry until the bottom sides are brown, about 5 minutes, then flip and brown the second side. Replenish the oil as needed, making sure the pan is hot before proceeding. Drain the latkes on paper towels and serve immediately.

Potato Latkes

MAKES 24 TO 30 LATKES

Lily Engelhardt serves these potato latkes on a large oval platter with a bowl of applesauce in the middle.

6 large potatoes, peeled and grated
  on medium holes of a box grater
2 eggs
1 medium onion, finely chopped
⅓ to ½ cup flour
1 tablespoon salt
Pepper to taste
Vegetable oil for frying

1. Thoroughly combine all the ingredients except the oil. Film the bottom of a large skillet with the oil and place over medium-high heat.
2. Working in batches, drop heaping tablespoonfuls of the potato mixture into the pan and flatten them slightly. Fry until the bottom sides are golden, about 4 minutes, then flip and brown the second sides. Replenish the oil as needed, making sure it is hot before proceeding. Drain the latkes on paper towels and serve immediately.

Homemade Applesauce

Latkes cry out for applesauce and fortunately Chanukah coincides with apple season. You can use any kind of apple to make applesauce, but mealy, even slightly bruised ones are particularly suitable.

Applesauce

5 pounds apples
1 cinnamon stick
Sugar

1. Cut the apples into eighths and place in a large kettle with water just to cover. Add cinnamon stick, cover and cook over medium heat until water boils.
2. Lower the heat and cook the apples at a slow simmer until they become soft and lose their shape; you can help them along with a wooden spoon or a potato masher. Stir occasionally so apples don't burn.
3. When the sauce has reached the desired consistency, add sugar to taste. When cool enough to handle, pass, in batches, through a food mill to remove seeds and bits of skin. Note: If you don't have a food mill, peel and core apples before cooking. Makes about 2 quarts.

Kahee (Fried Dough)

MAKES 12 SERVINGS

Lily Engelhardt makes her own puff pastry, but the frozen kind works just fine in this recipe.

¼ cup sugar
2 teaspoons cinnamon
1 (1-pound, 1-ounce) package frozen puff pastry
Vegetable oil for frying

1. Make cinnamon sugar by combining the sugar and cinnamon. Set aside.
2. Defrost the pastry according to package instructions. When pliable, place 1 sheet in the refrigerator and place the other on a well-floured work surface. Sprinkle the surface of the dough lightly with flour, then roll it out into a 12-by-18-inch rectangle. With a small, sharp knife, cut the dough into 6 (6-inch) circles and make a 2-inch slit in each circle to prevent the dough from bubbling when it's fried. Repeat with the second sheet of dough.
3. Heat ¼ inch of oil in a large skillet over medium-high heat. In batches, fry the circles in the oil until golden brown on one side, about 30 seconds, then turn and fry the second side until golden. Adjust the heat accordingly if the dough is cooking too quickly or too slowly. Drain the circles on paper towels and sprinkle immediately with the cinnamon sugar.

Lily Engelhardt helps the children with their menorahs: Tori Korine, Ross Engelhardt and Andrew Schwartz

Soufganioth (Chanukah Doughnuts)

MAKES 20 DOUGHNUTS

Soufganioth are as central to the Sephardic Chanukah celebration as latkes are to the Ashkenazic. Lily Engelhardt usually fills half of the batch with jam and leaves the other half plain.

1 package dried yeast (2½ teaspoons)
1 cup warm water
5 tablespoons plus 1 teaspoon sugar
2 eggs
2 egg yolks
½ cup (1 stick) margarine, softened
Pinch salt
1 teaspoon vanilla extract
2 tablespoons Cognac, optional
4 cups flour, plus more if necessary
Vegetable oil for deep-frying
½ cup strawberry, apricot, red currant or raspberry jam
Confectioners' sugar

1. Dissolve the yeast in the water with 1 teaspoon of the sugar and let sit until the mixture froths, about 10 minutes.
2. Beat the remaining sugar with the eggs and egg yolks. Add the margarine, salt, vanilla, Cognac, if using, and yeast mixture and beat well. Fold in the flour gradually, and continue beating until the dough is soft, smooth and elastic, adding a little more flour if necessary. Turn the dough out onto a lightly floured work surface and knead for 5 minutes. Place the dough in a bowl and cover with plastic wrap or a towel and leave in a warm place to rise for about 2 hours, or until doubled in bulk.
3. Turn the dough out on a lightly floured surface and knead it again, for 2 to 3 minutes. Using a floured rolling pin and working on a floured surface, roll the dough out to a thickness of ½ inch. Cut into 3-inch rounds using a pastry cutter. Place on floured wax or parchment paper, cover with a towel and let rise until doubled in bulk, 40 minutes to 1 hour.
4. Heat 2 inches of oil in a Dutch oven over high heat. The oil is ready when a piece of raw potato is dropped into the pot and the oil bubbles around it vigorously. Adjust the heat to medium-high and, place a few of the doughnuts in the oil. Fry until the underside is golden, 30 seconds to 1 minute, then turn and fry the second side. The total cooking time should be 1 to 2 minutes. Adjust the heat if the doughnuts are cooking too quickly or too slowly. Drain on paper towels and cool.
5. Fill a pastry bag fitted with a long, narrow tip with the jam. Jab the tip into each doughnut and fill with 1 teaspoon jam. Or, pierce each doughnut with a sharp knife and fill with jam using a small spoon. Before serving, sprinkle all the doughnuts with confectioners' sugar.

Tori Korine takes a doughnut from the dessert table while Shula Korine looks on.

CHRISTMAS EVE

Menu

Cold Seafood Salad
Shrimp Scampi
Baked Clams

Linguine With Shellfish Sauce
Hot Scungilli Over Pepper Biscuits
Calamari With White Garlic Sauce
Fried Calamari With Spicy Marinara Sauce
Broccoli Rabe

Ricotta Balls

The more courses the merrier

at an Italian-American family's

traditional Christmas Eve fete

A FEAST OF FISH

Ushering in Christmas with a grand seafood feast on the night before the holiday is one of the most cherished of Italian-American family traditions. But merely a lot of seafood won't do. There is a specific number of courses to which a family adheres year after year. What that number is, however, varies from family to family.

Seven, say those who serve seven fish dishes on Christmas Eve, signifies the seven sacraments, or the seven last words of Christ (or the seven virtues, or the seven days of the week). Nine-course adherents may arrive at that number by multiplying the Trinity by itself. Families who enjoy a 12-course dinner are honoring the 12 apostles, while those enjoying 11 courses are honoring the 12 apostles minus Judas, and those enjoying 13 courses are honoring the 12 apostles plus Christ.

According to Father James Vlaun, chaplain at St. John the Baptist Diocesan High School in West Islip and a veteran of many Christmas Eve feasts, the orig-

Opposite, Micki
Cangemi chats with
her husband, Joseph,
and her mother-in-law,
Vincenza Cangemi.
Right, hot scungilli over
pepper biscuits.

16

inal practitioners of the "Vigilia di Natale" probably first came up with the idea of a big meal and then provided the liturgical justification for the number of courses.

Michelina and Joseph Cangemi of Hicksville follow the 12-dishes-for-12-apostles line. The first courses are baccala (salt cod) salad, seafood salad, baked clams and shrimp scampi. Then the family moves on to the main dishes: linguine with shellfish sauce, fried breaded shrimp, baked baccala, spicy scungilli (conch) over pepper biscuits, fried eels, calamari with garlic sauce and fried calamari with spicy marinara sauce, accompanied by broccoli rabe.

When the dishes are cleared, a tray of raw fennel and celery hearts is passed, but this brief foray into spa cuisine is soon overtaken by the onslaught of dessert: cream puffs, fried ricotta balls, assorted pastries, mixed nuts, roasted chestnuts, fresh fruit, dried fruit and Perugina Baci. Liqueur is served in tiny dark-chocolate cups, followed by espresso, coffee and tea.

Four generations gather each year at the Cangemis' Christmas-bedecked house. There are Michelina's parents, Gaetano and Annunziata Odierno; Joseph's mother, Vincenza Cangemi, and the host couple's four children, their spouses and the three grandchildren. Throw in assorted cousins, in-laws and neighbors and soon there are 24 people, all of whom Micki (Michelina) serves in Yuletide style with her extensive collection of Christmas china and stemware.

The family sits down to dinner early on Christmas Eve, "and we don't finish until we're through," said Gaetano Odierno. Around 9 p.m., friends and neighbors start dropping by to sample the bounty and at 11:30 many of the diners head off to midnight mass. The stay-at-homes clean up, rest, play board games and continue noshing. When the church-goers return, the family members resume their places at the table for the post-mass repast, broiled sausages and "the mess," family shorthand for Annunziata's spicy melange of escarole, broccoli, cabbage, cannellini beans and cubed day-old bread that accompanies the sausage.

"And don't forget," added Micki, "all the dessert is still on the table. And with this crowd, they're not above going back into the kitchen for more fish."

Preparing Scungilli

An important part of the Christmas Eve meal is the laborious preparation that goes into it. One particularly challenging task is preparing scungilli, or conch, easily found at Christmastime at fish stores that cater to an Italian clientele. Micki Cangemi's daughter, Vicki Ahlsen, is a life-sciences teacher and she brings all her scientific expertise to bear on the knobby little mottled creatures that look, to the uninitiated, like an unlikely basis for a special holiday dish.

"We buy it out of the shell, parboiled," Vicki explained, adding that they never purchase it canned. "First we trim all the black parts, then we cut off the little...my mother-in-law calls it the 'zootzik,' the little flaps." Next the trimmed knobs are sliced into medallions, the darker pieces slated for the red-sauced pepper biscuits, the smaller, whiter ones for the seafood salad.

Cold Seafood Salad
MAKES 15 TO 20 SERVINGS
Micki Cangemi serves the leftover salad on Christmas Day.

2½ pounds shrimp (16 to 20 per pound), cleaned and deveined
4 pounds calamari, cleaned, with heads sliced into rings, tentacles left whole or, if unappetizingly long, cut in half
2 pounds scungilli, cleaned, dark areas and flappy bits trimmed, then cut into bite-sized pieces
1 (1-pound, 1.3-ounce) can frozen lobster meat, thawed
2 cups sliced celery
1 cup lemon juice
⅓ cup extra-virgin olive oil
½ head garlic, chopped
Crushed red pepper to taste
Salt and pepper to taste
1 (1-pound) can fresh crabmeat

Boil the shrimp and calamari separately until firm, 4 to 6 minutes for the shrimp, not more than 5 minutes for the calamari. Place in a large mixing bowl and add the remaining ingredients except for the crabmeat and toss well. Pick over the crabmeat to remove any pieces of shell or cartilage. Toss with the rest of the salad. Refrigerate until chilled, then serve.

Baked Clams

MAKES 8 SERVINGS

Micki Cangemi uses high-quality canned clams for this dish. But if you want to use fresh, substitute 16 large clams, shucked and chopped, plus their liquid.

2 tablespoons vegetable oil
1 small onion, finely minced
2 cloves garlic, finely minced
2 tablespoons chopped parsley
¼ teaspoon dried oregano
½ cup unseasoned bread crumbs
¼ teaspoon salt
2 (8-ounce) cans minced clams
16 clam shells (available at fish markets)
Parmesan cheese
Paprika
Lemon wedges

Heat the oil over medium heat and saute the onion until translucent. Add the garlic and saute until it just begins to brown. Blend in the parsley, oregano, bread crumbs and salt, and remove from heat. Add the clams and their juice. Stuff the shells with the mixture, then sprinkle on cheese and paprika. Bake at 375 degrees for 20 minutes, until golden brown on top. Serve with lemon wedges.

Shrimp Scampi

MAKES 12 SERVINGS

When making shrimp scampi, Micki Cangemi says that the shellfish should be taken off the heat before the cold butter is added, otherwise the sauce will thin out and separate.

Olive oil for sauteing
2½ pounds shrimp (16 to 20 per pound), cleaned, deveined, butterflied, with tails on
5 cloves garlic, chopped
½ cup white wine
Juice of 2 lemons
4 tablespoons (½ stick) cold butter
¼ cup chopped parsley

1. Coat a large skillet with olive oil and place over high heat. Saute the shrimp in batches, if necessary, until just pink and cooked through, about 2 to 3 minutes. Remove the shrimp from the pan. Add the garlic and saute until golden.
2. Drain the excess oil and deglaze the pan with the wine and lemon juice. Return the shrimp to the pan and simmer 2 minutes. Remove from the heat and add the cold butter a little at a time so that sauce thickens. Stir in the parsley. Serve immediately.

Linguine With Shellfish Sauce

MAKES 12 SERVINGS

Micki Cangemi plates individual servings of this dish in the kitchen, topping each one with an extra clam or mussel. Then she puts a large bowl of linguine topped with sauce on the table, plus gravy boats with extra sauce.

Vegetable oil for sauteing
6 cloves garlic, chopped
3 (6-ounce) cans tomato paste
Salt and pepper to taste
3 (28-ounce) cans whole tomatoes, pureed
6 (3- to 4-ounce) frozen Maine lobster tails, thawed
2 dozen littleneck clams, cleaned
2 pounds mussels, cleaned
3 pounds linguine

1. Coat a large skillet with oil and place over high heat. Saute the garlic until golden. Add the tomato paste, salt and pepper. Mix thoroughly. Add 3 tomato paste cans of water. Stir and bring to a simmer. Add the pureed tomatoes, bring to a boil, and add 1½ tomato cans of water. Bring to a boil, then lower to a simmer and cook, uncovered, 2 hours, stirring often until sauce has thickened but doesn't stick to the bottom of the pan. (If it does, thin it out with a little water.)
2. Add the shellfish to the sauce and return to a simmer. Cook until the lobster tails are hot and the clams and mussels have opened. Discard any clams or mussels that do not open. Remove the lobster tails and split them, then return them to the sauce.
3. Meanwhile, cook the linguine until al dente according to package instructions. Drain, place in large serving bowl and top with the fish sauce.

Hot Scungilli Over Pepper Biscuits

MAKES 12 SERVINGS

Pepper biscuits, the thick rusks known in Italian as friscelle, can be found at most Italian specialty stores.

Vegetable oil to coat pan
3 cloves garlic, whole
2 tablespoons crushed red pepper flakes or to taste
3 (12-ounce) cans tomato paste
Salt and pepper to taste
3 pounds scungilli, cleaned, dark areas and flappy bits trimmed, then sliced into thin medallions
1 (12-ounce) bag pepper biscuits

1. Coat a large pot or Dutch oven with oil. Brown the garlic until dark brown, almost black. Remove from the pan and discard. Add the red pepper flakes and stir for 20 seconds. Add the tomato paste and stir in 6 tomato paste cans of water. Add salt and pepper and bring to a boil. Lower the heat and simmer, uncovered, for 2 hours, stirring often, until the sauce has thickened but doesn't stick to the bottom of the pan. (If it does, thin it with a little water.) Add scungilli and cook 10 more minutes to blend flavors.
2. A few minutes before the dish finishes cooking, dip the biscuits quickly in water to slightly soften them. Place the biscuits in 1 layer in the bottom of 1 large or 2 medium platters. Pour the sauce over the biscuits and serve.

Christina and Gregory Ahlsen open gifts while, from left, their grandmother, Micki Cangemi, and great grandparents Annunziata and Gaetano Odierno and Vincenza Cangemi look on.

Calamari With White Garlic Sauce

MAKES 12 SERVINGS

The trick to cooking calamari is to cook it very quickly or for a long time. Any length of time in between, it gets unpalatably tough. Micki Cangemi favors the long method for this recipe.

4 pounds calamari, cleaned and sliced into rings, tentacles left whole unless unappetizingly long
Olive oil to coat pan
3 cloves garlic, sliced
2 tablespoons chopped parsley
2 ounces red wine vinegar
Salt and pepper to taste

Place all the ingredients in a large saucepan and stir to combine. Bring to a boil, lower the heat and simmer until the calamari is done, about 40 minutes.

Fried Calamari

MAKES 12 SERVINGS

Most fishmongers (and many supermarkets) sell cleaned squid, saving you the trouble of cleaning it yourself.

5 pounds cleaned squid
2 to 3 cups vegetable oil for deep frying
2 cups flour
Salt and pepper to taste
Lemon wedges
Spicy marinara sauce (recipe follows)

1. Slice the squid bodies into rings about ½ inch wide and break the tentacles into bite-size clusters. Pat dry.
2. Place the vegetable oil in a large pot and heat to 375 degrees.
3. Combine the flour, salt and pepper in a large shallow platter. When the oil is hot, dredge a handful of the calamari pieces in the flour, shake off the excess and drop into hot oil. (The oil should bubble vigorously around the pieces.) Do not fry too many pieces at one time or oil will cool.
4. When the first side of the calamari is a golden brown, turn with a slotted spoon or Chinese "spider" and fry the second side until golden brown, 3 to 4 minutes total. Remove from the oil and drain on paper towels. Serve immediately with lemon wedges and spicy marinara sauce.

NanciAnn Cangemi and Gregg Ahlsen serve themselves.

Spicy Marinara Sauce

MAKES ABOUT 5 CUPS

This recipes makes more sauce then you may need for the fried calamari, but it is equally good with other fried seafood or, cooled, with shrimp cocktail.

2 (28-ounce) cans whole tomatoes
Olive oil to coat pan
6 cloves garlic, minced
Salt
Red pepper flakes

Pour the tomatoes into a bowl and break them up with your hands. Pour a thin film of olive oil into a large, deep skillet or saucepan. Add the garlic and saute over medium heat until it just begins to turn brown. Add the tomatoes to the pan with 1 tomato can of water. Bring to a boil, then lower the heat so the sauce simmers slowly. Cook until the sauce is just thick enough to cling to the fried calamari. Add salt and red pepper flakes to taste.

Broccoli Rabe

MAKES 12 SERVINGS

As opposed to some of the "Christmas only" seafood recipes here, the Cangemis eat this broccoli rabe throughout the year.

4 pounds broccoli rabe, washed and drained
Extra-virgin olive oil
4 to 6 cloves garlic, sliced
Salt and pepper

1. Trim the stems of the broccoli rabe where the leaves start and discard them.
2. Coat the surface of a very large skillet with olive oil. (Unless your skillet is large enough to fit all the broccoli rabe in 1 layer, use 2 skillets.) Saute the garlic until golden brown over high heat. Add the broccoli rabe and salt and pepper to taste, and cover. Reduce the heat to medium high and cook until the broccoli rabe is tender, about 15 minutes.

"The Mess"

When the Cangemi clan returns from midnight mass, they have already somehow managed to work up an appetite. There's plenty of leftover seafood, of course, but the main event of this meal is "the mess," the specialty of Micki Cangemi's mother, Annunziata Odierno. It is usually served alongside broiled sausages.

1 medium head escarole, coarsely cut
1 small head cabbage, cut into 1-inch slices
1 bunch broccoli
Olive oil
4 cloves garlic, minced
Red pepper flakes to taste
1 (15-ounce) can cannellini beans
Salt and pepper
1 day-old loaf Italian bread, cut into large chunks

1. Bring a large pot of salted water to boil. Blanch escarole and cabbage until just tender, but not soft; they will cook fully later. With a slotted spoon, remove escarole and cabbage from water. Keep water boiling.
2. Cut off bottom inch of stalk from broccoli and peel remaining stalk if desired. Cut broccoli stalk and florets into walnut-sized pieces. Blanch broccoli in boiling water until just tender. Drain, reserving a cup or so of cooking water.
3. Coat bottom of large skillet with olive oil. Add garlic and over medium heat, cook until it just starts to brown. Add red pepper flakes, drained vegetables and the beans along with their liquid. Add salt and pepper to taste, then simmer, partially covered, over low heat for 10 to 15 minutes, or until vegetables are fully cooked, adding reserved cooking liquid if mixture dries out.
4. Just before serving, add bread to skillet, stirring gently. Cook until bread has absorbed most of the liquid, again adding more reserved broccoli cooking water if mixture is too dry. Makes 8 to 10 servings.

Ricotta Balls

MAKES 12 SERVINGS

Fried dough is almost synonymous with Italian celebration desserts.

1 pound ricotta cheese
1 tablespoon baking powder
1 teaspoon vanilla extract
3 eggs
1 cup flour
2 cups vegetable oil for deep frying
Confectioners' sugar for dusting

Combine the ricotta, baking powder, vanilla, eggs and flour, and mix well. In a deep fryer or large pot, heat the oil to 375 degrees. Working in batches, drop teaspoonful-size balls of dough into the oil and fry until golden brown, 2 to 3 minutes, turning them once. Drain on paper towels. Sprinkle with confectioners' sugar while hot and serve immediately.

Above, from left, Annunziata Odierno and Vincenza Cangemi sample the first batch of ricotta balls.

CHRISTMAS

Menu

Cranberry Compote
Mustard-Glazed Ham
Kielbasa and Sauerkraut
Grandpa Al's Potatoes
Mushroom Soup With Dill
Asparagus With Lemon
Pirohi

Eggnog
Two-Hour Nut Roll
Braided Yeast Bread

In a neighborhood strong with traditions, a tight-knit family draws upon a rich culinary heritage

TASTE OF THE OLD WORLD

Christmas is a special time on Lincoln Avenue — a short street of tidy homes near the train station in Massapequa Park. Residents such as Tom and Ann Fermature, who have lived there for decades, open their homes to their neighbors for good food and good cheer. Even Santa makes regular visits to the children, thanks to one neighbor whose family members have played St. Nick for two generations.

"He was the most beautiful Santa," said Amanda Fermature, one of the Fermatures' three grown daughters, when remembering the late John Busemi in his red velvet costume and professionally made white wig and beard. "He would throw rocks on our roof at about 10 or 11 p.m. and wake us up. Then we'd run downstairs and let him in and he would give us our presents." Busemi's daughter, Theresa Anderson, still lives on Lincoln Avenue, and now her brother, John Busemi, Jr., carries on the tradition.

The neighbors on Lincoln Avenue are an admittedly tight-knit and tradition-bound group. The open houses of Christmas give way in summer to annual

Ann Fermature serves ham to neighbor Edie Zuzolo, left, and daughter Amanda, right.

block parties — all-day affairs with disc jockeys, volleyball and games set up on front lawns so that the children can move from house to house.

Claudia Allard, another Fermature daughter, said, "Most of these men and women grew up the children of immigrants. They don't want to lose that togetherness you have when you live in a little immigrant community like Yorkville. That's how they survived. I've lived in so many places — Seattle, Washington, D.C., Atlanta, Maryland — but nothing compares with Lincoln Avenue."

Ann and Tom grew up in the Yorkville section of Manhattan, where Ann learned to make Slovak favorites such as *pirohi*, which most people know as Polish pierogi, a dumpling stuffed with potato or cheese; *orzky*, a cookie similar to rugelach; *bozhi milosti*, a deep-fried dough sprinkled with powdered sugar, and *flicky*, a noodle-and-ham casserole made with the leftovers from Christmas dinner.

It has been 35 years since the couple left Yorkville for Massapequa Park, but Ann keeps the tradition alive, particularly at Christmastime. Her daughters count her Slovak dishes as their holiday favorites, especially the nut roll, pirohi and the flicky. "You know what's nice?" said daughter Michele Fermature. "None of it changes and none of us changes."

Buying Ham

Buying a fully cooked ham involves making many choices. There is bone-in vs. boneless, whole vs. half, butt vs. shank end. Here's what you need to know about cooked hams.

• A whole ham, 10 to 12 pounds, will serve 20 people with leftovers, while a half, 5 to 6 pounds, will do for 10 to 12 people.

• A boneless ham is easier to slice, but many people believe that a bone-in ham is worth the extra trouble because it is more flavorful. Likewise, a butt is meatier than a shank end, but is more difficult to carve.

• When shopping for a fully cooked supermarket ham, read the fine print. Not all hams are created equal. A product labeled "ham" is the best and most expensive choice. It contains no extra water and is at least 20.5 percent protein. "Ham with natural juices" contains at least 18.5 percent protein. "Ham with water added" contains more water and at least 17 percent protein. A ham labeled "ham and water product" contains the least amount of protein and subsequently is the least expensive.

Mustard-Glazed Ham

MAKES 10 SERVINGS, OR 20

The Fermatures treat themselves to a store-bought, honey-glazed ham at Christmas. But it's simple enough to make at home.

1 cooked ham of your choice, whole or half,
   bone-in or boneless
¼ cup Dijon mustard
¼ cup packed light or dark brown sugar

1. Preheat the oven to 325 degrees. Line a shallow roasting pan with aluminum foil. Cut away any excess skin from the ham and trim the fat to a thickness of ¼ to ½ inch. Place the ham, fat side up, in the foil-lined roasting pan.

2. Place the ham in preheated oven and bake. Using an instant-read meat thermometer, check the temperature of a whole ham after 2 hours and a half ham after 1 hour. When the thermometer registers between 130 and 140 degrees (because the ham was precooked, it only needs to be heated through) remove the ham from the oven.

3. Increase the oven temperature to 425 degrees. Score the surface of the ham to make a criss-cross grid. Mix the mustard and sugar in a bowl (double the amounts above for a whole ham), and spread generously over the ham. Return it to the oven and bake for 20 minutes more, occasionally basting it with the pan juices. Brush on more glaze, if desired.

4. Remove the ham from the oven and cover it loosely with foil. Let it rest for about 30 minutes before carving. A half ham makes about 10 servings, a whole ham makes about 20.

Flicky

One of the best ways to use leftovers from Christmas dinner is this traditional Slovak noodle and ham casserole called flicky.

1 (12-ounce) package egg noodles
¼ cup butter
1 pound ham or smoked meat, diced
3 eggs, lightly beaten
1 cup milk
Salt to taste

Preheat the oven to 350 degrees. Prepare the egg noodles according to package instructions. Drain. Mix with the butter and ham. Put into a well-greased casserole. Mix the eggs, milk and salt and pour over the noodles. Bake for 30 to 45 minutes or until eggs are set. Makes 4 servings.

Cranberry Compote

MAKES 12 SERVINGS

The Fermature daughters like this cranberry side dish so much that they make compote sandwiches with the leftovers the day after Christmas.

¾ cup water
½ cup brandy, preferably apple
¾ cup sugar
3 firm pears, peeled, cored and diced
4 cups (1-pound) fresh cranberries, rinsed
1 cup chunky applesauce
1 cup crushed pineapple or pineapple chunks, drained
¾ cup toasted walnuts, coarsely chopped
1 (11-ounce) can mandarin oranges

1. In a large saucepan, bring the water, brandy and sugar to a boil and stir until the sugar is dissolved. Add the pears, reduce heat and simmer uncovered for 5 minutes.

2. Add the cranberries and continue to cook over medium heat until the berries have popped and the mixture starts to thicken, about 5 minutes.

3. Remove the mixture from the heat and stir in the applesauce, pineapple, walnuts and mandarin oranges.

Kielbasa and Sauerkraut

MAKES 12 SERVINGS

Kielbasa can be bought fresh in a specialty butcher shop or smoked in the supermarket.

½ cup butter
2 medium onions, diced
2 pounds sauerkraut
1 teaspoon caraway seeds
3 pounds cooked kielbasa
3 tablespoons flour
2 tablespoons sugar
Salt to taste
½ cup white wine or water

1. In a large saute pan, melt the butter. Add the onions and saute them until they are browned, about 10 minutes. Add the sauerkraut and caraway seeds and continue to cook the mixture until the sauerkraut is tender, about 30 minutes.
2. Meanwhile, in another saute pan, cook the kielbasa over medium heat until warmed through, about 10 minutes.
3. When the sauerkraut is tender, sprinkle it with the flour, sugar and salt. Stir in the wine or water, and simmer uncovered for 5 minutes more. To serve, place the sauerkraut on a serving platter and set the kielbasa on top.

Grandpa Al's Potatoes

MAKES 12 SERVINGS

4 pounds potatoes (about 8 medium to large)
½ cup butter, divided
½ cup chopped onion
1 (10¾-ounce) can cream of chicken or
  cream of mushroom soup
1 pint sour cream
1½ cups shredded Cheddar cheese
½ cup crushed corn flakes cereal

1. In a large pot, parboil the potatoes with the skins on until just tender but still firm inside, about 20 minutes. Remove from the water and set aside. When cool enough to handle, peel and grate the potatoes. Set aside.
2. Preheat the oven to 350 degrees. In a saute pan, heat ¼ cup butter and cook the onions over medium heat until brown, about 10 minutes. Stir in the soup, sour cream and cheese and heat through, stirring constantly.
3. Spread the potatoes in a greased, 9-by-13-inch dish and pour the cheese mixture over, mixing slightly. Sprinkle the crushed corn flakes on top and dot with pats of the remaining butter. Bake until bubbly and golden brown on top, about 45 minutes to 1 hour.

Mushroom Soup With Dill

MAKES 12 SERVINGS

Mushroom soup is part of the simple meal that the Fermatures share on Christmas Eve. This satisfying soup is a rich addition for Christmas dinner as well.

½ cup butter
1½ cups onions, finely chopped
1 pound fresh mushrooms, sliced
4½ tablespoons flour
8 cups (2 quarts) beef stock or broth
2 teaspoons salt
Freshly ground black pepper
½ cup milk
1 cup sour cream, at room temperature
Several sprigs of fresh dill

1. In a large pot, melt the butter over medium-high heat. Add the onions and cook until translucent. Add the mushrooms and saute until limp. Add the flour and cook, whisking constantly until the mixture browns, about 3 minutes.
2. Slowly pour in the stock or broth, scraping up any browned bits from the bottom of the pan. Season to taste with salt and pepper, and simmer for 10 minutes. Set the soup aside to cool slightly.
3. Add the milk and warm the soup until it begins to simmer. Ladle into individual bowls and top each serving with a dollop of sour cream and a few sprigs of dill.

Asparagus With Lemon

MAKES 8 TO 10 SERVINGS

2 pounds asparagus, trimmed and peeled
1 to 2 tablespoons butter
Fresh lemon juice to taste
Salt and freshly ground pepper to taste

1. Place the asparagus in a large saute pan, add ½ inch water and cover. Bring to a boil and then promptly turn off heat. Keep covered and check with a fork until it has reached desired doneness.
2. When the asparagus is done, drain. Then toss with the butter and lemon juice until all of the spears are thoroughly coated. Season with salt and pepper.

Pirohi

MAKES 10 SERVINGS

Pirohi, otherwise known as pierogi, are Slovak dumplings.

For the dough:
2 cups flour
2 eggs, lightly beaten
½ teaspoon salt
For the filling:
1 large potato, cooked, peeled and mashed
1 tablespoon butter, softened
½ teaspoon salt
¼ cup butter, melted

1. Mix the flour, eggs and salt. Add enough water to make a medium-soft dough, about ¼ cup. Knead the dough until blisters appear. Dough should be soft. Cover and let rest for 1 hour.
2. On a floured work surface, divide the dough in half and roll each portion into a rectangle ¼ inch thick. With a sharp knife or pastry cutter, cut each rectangle into 2-inch squares.
3. To make the filling, mix the potato, 1 tablespoon butter and salt. Place 1 tablespoon filling in center of each square. Fold in half to form triangles, pinching edges.
4. Working with ⅓ of the batch at a time, drop the dumplings into boiling salted water and cook until the pirohi rise to the surface, about 10 minutes. Drain the dumplings.
5. Meanwhile, brown the remaining ¼ cup butter in a skillet. Add the dumplings and toss just before serving.

Holiday Eggnog

Colonial Americans are thought to have created the `libation as a derivation of European punch made from milk and wine. Because this recipe uses raw eggs, it is best to use pasteurized ones.

9 large egg yolks
¾ cup granulated sugar
2 cups heavy cream
1 cup whole milk
¾ cup bourbon
¾ cup dark rum
Freshly grated nutmeg, for garnish

Using an electric mixer on high speed, beat egg yolks and sugar until they are pale and thickened, about 3 minutes. Gradually beat in cream, milk, bourbon and rum. Cover and refrigerate until chilled, about 3 hours. Garnish with nutmeg. Makes 8 to 10 servings.

Two-Hour Nut Roll

MAKES 4 LOAVES

If any single food means Christmas to the Fermature family, this nut roll is it.

For the dough:
4 packets dry yeast
½ cup warm milk
½ pound butter, softened
3 tablespoons sugar
1 cup sour cream
3 eggs
6 cups sifted flour
1 teaspoon salt
For the filling:
2 cups sugar
1 pound walnuts, toasted and finely chopped
1 egg, for glaze

1. Dissolve the yeast in the warmed milk. Set aside until the yeast is bubbly.
2. Cream the butter and sugar. Add the sour cream and 3 eggs, and stir to combine. Stir in the yeast mixture. Combine the flour and salt and incorporate the mixture ½ cup at a time into the previous ingredients.
3. Turn the mixture out onto a floured work surface and knead. Divide the dough into 4 parts. Roll each part into a rectangle measuring 7-by-12-inches and ¼ inch thick.
4. Make the filling by mixing the sugar and walnuts.
5. Spread ¼ of the filling over each rectangle, leaving a 1-inch border around the edges. Roll the dough, jelly-roll style, starting at the long side of the rectangle. Tuck the ends under the roll to seal. Pat each roll gently to make sure the filling adheres to the dough.
6. Place the rolls seam-side down on greased baking sheets and allow them to rise for 1 hour at room temperature, or until doubled in bulk. Mix the remaining egg with 2 tablespoons water and brush on the loaves. Heat the oven to 350 degrees and bake the loaves for 35 to 40 minutes, or until golden.

Braided Yeast Bread

MAKES 2 LOAVES

Here is another of the Fermatures' favorite holiday treats.

2 packets dry yeast
½ cup warm water
½ cup butter or margarine, softened
½ cup sugar
1 teaspoon salt
Zest of 1 lemon
1 cup milk
6 cups flour, divided
4 egg yolks
1 whole egg
1 cup chopped candied fruit or raisins
1 egg white
½ cup sliced almonds

1. Dissolve the yeast in warm water mixed with a pinch of the sugar. Set aside.

2. In another bowl, combine the butter or margarine, sugar, salt and lemon rind. Scald the milk in a saucepan by bringing to a boil and remove from heat immediately. Pour into the butter mixture. Stir until the butter melts, then let cool until the mixture is lukewarm.

3. Add 2 cups of the flour and the yeast to the butter mixture and mix well. Set aside until bubbly.

4. Stir the egg yolks and the whole egg into the mixture and gradually beat in the remaining 4 cups of flour, until the dough is soft and light. Turn the dough out onto a floured work surface and knead until smooth. Shape the dough into a ball and place in a floured bowl and cover with a towel. Let it rise for 1 to 1½ hours, or until doubled in size.

5. Punch down the dough and turn it onto a lightly floured work surface. Knead in the candied fruit or raisins. Let the dough rest for 10 minutes, then divide it into two pieces. Cut each half into thirds. Gently stretch the pieces into lengths of dough. On a baking sheet, braid three of the lengths to form a loaf. Repeat with remaining three lengths. Brush the top of each loaf with the egg white and sprinkle with the sliced almonds.

6. Bake in a preheated 350-degree oven for 20 to 25 minutes or until the loaves are golden brown.

Tom Fermature, center, and his daughters Amanda, left, and Michele, right, relax with their friends and family.

CHAPTER VI

KWANZAA

Menu

Kwanzaa Fried Chicken
Groundnut Stew
Palava Sauce
Macaroni and Cheese
Mildred Clayton's Yams
Collard Greens

Kwanzaa Cookies
Cornmeal Pie

A feast of

African and Southern foods

honors a proud heritage

A CULINARY JOURNEY

Tradition, ritual, togetherness and good food: These are the essential ingredients that make up any holiday. And while Kwanzaa might not be a very old holiday, it is, to an increasing number of African American families, one that's rich in the things that matter.

The first Kwanzaa celebration occurred in 1966, when Maulana Karenga, a California professor of black studies, harked back to the African tradition of giving thanks for the first fruits of the harvest. For seven days, from Dec. 26 to Jan. 1, folks get together to light the *kinara*, a symbolic candelabra, and celebrate a bountiful cultural heritage.

It is with that heritage in mind that Mildred Clayton invites family members and friends into her Westbury home each Kwanzaa. Mildred, an interpreter at the African American Museum in Hempstead, likes to include a large contingent of young people, many of them members of her church and community choirs.

Mildred's son, Larinzo, a lawyer who lives in Freeport, welcomes the group with a traditional Swahili greeting.

Second from left, Larinzo Clayton looks on with other guests as Kivira Mack lights the khuara.

Then there is a spirited session of poetry readings and musical performances. Afterwards everyone gathers around the Kwanzaa table, where fruit spills from a horn of plenty. The young people take turns lighting the candles, which represent the principles of Kwanzaa — unity, self-determination, collective work, cooperative economics, purpose, creativity and faith. Gifts, which must be homemade or educational, are exchanged. At last, it's time to partake of the savory fare intrinsic to the African American experience.

In the spirit of Kwanzaa, which celebrates the struggles and the triumphs of African Americans over the years, the food that is served has its roots in history. There's the fare of the American South: Mildred cooks up lots of fried chicken from a cherished family recipe. There's also creamy macaroni and cheese and collard greens seasoned with ham hocks. Roast turkey is a must, served with corn on the cob, which symbolizes family and children.

And then, there's the food of Africa. Shirley Darkeh, a Westbury resident whose husband George hails from Ghana, brings African groundnut stew, made with peanut butter, and *palava*, a lush fish and vegetable sauce that is ladled over rice.

Pearlie Mae Tubbs of Westbury, an ordained minister known affectionately as Mother Tubbs, comes with her light and custardy cornmeal pie. There's also sweet potato pie and Kwanzaa cookies, made with peanut butter and decorated primarily in the colors of Kwanzaa — red, green and black.

But Kwanzaa is a feast not only of food but of inspiration, especially for the younger guests. Larinzo Clayton tells them, "Live your lives with purpose, not haphazardly."

Kwanzaa Fried Chicken

MAKES 4 SERVINGS

This is an exceptionally flavorsome fried chicken. It was contained in a book of recipes compiled for a family reunion Mildred Clayton attended.

¼ cup hot sauce
1 tablespoon yellow mustard
1 (3-pound) chicken, cut into pieces
1 cup flour
1 tablespoon cornmeal
¼ cup Italian bread crumbs
Vegetable oil for frying

1. Combine the hot sauce and mustard. Coat the chicken in the mixture and allow to marinate about 10 minutes.
2. Combine the flour, cornmeal and bread crumbs; dredge the chicken in the mixture.
3. Fry over medium heat in a heavy-bottomed skillet in about 1 to 2 inches of hot oil, turning frequently, until the chicken is golden brown on both sides and an instant-read thermometer inserted into meat (without touching a bone) reads 160 to 165 degrees, about 17 to 20 minutes.

**Denise Moleah and
her daughter, Nosizwe**

Groundnut Stew

MAKES 4 SERVINGS

This lively African peanut stew may also be made using chicken legs or cubed lamb.

3 tablespoons vegetable oil, divided
2 pounds cubed stew beef
1 large onion, chopped
2 cups chicken stock or broth
½ cup creamy peanut butter
3 tablespoons tomato paste
2 large tomatoes, peeled and chopped
2 teaspoons salt
1 teaspoon black pepper

1. In a heavy-bottomed skillet, heat 2 tablespoons of the oil. Add ⅓ of the beef, sear until brown on all sides, and remove to a heavy-bottomed Dutch oven. Continue to brown the remaining beef in batches.
2. In the same skillet, heat the remaining oil. Add the onions and saute until golden. Stir in the chicken stock, peanut butter and tomato paste. Pour over the beef in the Dutch oven, adding the chopped tomatoes, salt and pepper.
3. Simmer over low heat for about 2 hours or until the beef is tender. Serve with rice.

Palava Sauce

MAKES 4 SERVINGS

This fish and vegetable sauce (more of a stew) is a Kwanzaa tradition for Shirley Darkeh of Westbury. The sauce has its origins in Ghana, where Shirley's husband George was born.

2 tablespoons oil
1 large onion, chopped
4 large tomatoes, peeled and chopped
1 (15-ounce) can tomato sauce
4 jalapeño peppers, seeded and chopped
¼ teaspoon cayenne pepper
1 teaspoon salt
1½ pounds salmon, cut in 1½-inch cubes
¼ pound smoked or kippered herring
   (or other smoked fish), finely chopped
2 (10-ounce) packages frozen chopped spinach, thawed

In a large saute pan, heat the oil. Add the onions and saute until golden. Add the tomatoes, tomato sauce, jalapeños and seasonings. Add the fish, cover, and simmer 20 minutes. Add the spinach and warm through. Serve with rice.

Macaroni and Cheese

MAKES 4 MAIN COURSE SERVINGS, 8 SIDE DISH

Mildred Clayton's macaroni and cheese is a true comfort food that's a favorite of both children and adults.

1 (16-ounce) box elbow macaroni
4 tablespoons (½ stick) butter
½ cup flour
2 cups warmed milk
4 eggs, beaten
2 teaspoons salt
1 teaspoon pepper
8 ounces shredded Cheddar cheese
4 to 6 ounces sliced Cheddar cheese

1. Boil the macaroni until slightly undercooked according to package instructions. Drain and rinse.
2. In a saucepan over medium heat, melt the butter. Stir in the flour and cook a few seconds. Then, whisk in the milk, stirring until smooth. Remove from heat. When the mixture has cooled, whisk in the eggs, salt and pepper.
3. Preheat the oven to 350 degrees. In a large, buttered casserole, layer the macaroni and shredded cheese, making 3 layers. Pour on the milk and egg mixture. Top with the sliced Cheddar. Bake 30 to 40 minutes.

Mildred Clayton's Yams

MAKES 10 TO 12 SERVINGS

The yam is a root vegetable used in African cooking as well as in southern cuisine. Mildred Clayton's recipe combines brown sugar and spice with a hint of citrus and a tropical accent of coconut.

10 medium yams or sweet potatoes (about 6 pounds), peeled
1 cup (2 sticks) butter
1½ cups brown sugar
1 (7-ounce) package shredded coconut
2½ teaspoons lemon juice
1 tablespoon cinnamon
1 tablespoon vanilla extract
1 teaspoon ginger
½ teaspoon allspice
1 cup orange juice
Orange slices for garnish

1. Preheat the oven to 350 degrees.
2. Parboil the yams until they can be easily pierced with the tip of a knife. Drain. When the yams are cool enough to handle, cut into ½-inch slices. Set aside.
3. In a saucepan, melt the butter and add the remaining ingredients except the orange slices. Heat until warm and smooth.
4. Place the yams in a large, deep, buttered casserole and pour the sauce over. Bake about 30 minutes. Garnish with the orange slices.

Collard Greens

MAKES 6 SERVINGS

For many African American families, no holiday would be complete without collard greens. This is Mildred's recipe.

4 strips bacon, cut into 1-inch pieces
1 to 2 pounds cut-up smoked turkey legs or wings
2 pounds ham hocks
4 quarts roughly chopped collard greens,
   thoroughly cleaned, stems discarded
2 to 3 tablespoons sugar
½ teaspoon baking soda for color maintenance, optional

1. In a heavy-bottomed stockpot, cook the bacon until golden. Add the turkey, ham hocks and collard greens. Cover with water. Simmer until the greens are tender, about 1½ to 2 hours, adding water as needed (there should be a generous amount of liquid around the greens).
2. Add the sugar and baking soda; cook an additional 15 minutes. Remove the turkey and ham hocks and serve.

From left, Trenné O'Neil, Alvita Mack, Melissa O'Neil, Tyrone Ashford and Joynelle Carr take turns singing during the celebration.

Kwanzaa Cookies

MAKES 35 TO 40 COOKIES

These colorful iced cookies brighten any Kwanzaa table. If you are pressed for time, a commercial icing may be substituted for the homemade one used here.

½ cup (1 stick) unsalted butter, softened
⅔ cup sugar
1 egg
½ teaspoon vanilla extract
½ cup creamy peanut butter
1½ cups flour
½ teaspoon salt
½ teaspoon baking soda
For the icing:
2 cups confectioners' sugar
1 teaspoon vanilla extract
8 to 10 tablespoons heavy cream
Few drops food coloring in red, yellow, green, purple and black

1. Preheat the oven to 350 degrees.

2. Cream together the butter and sugar until smooth. Add the egg and vanilla, beating until smooth. Add the peanut butter; blend well. Blend in the flour, salt and baking soda.

3. Roll out the dough on a floured board until ¼ inch thick. Using a 2¼-inch circular cookie cutter, cut out cookies. Bake on a cookie sheet in the preheated oven until barely golden, 8 to 10 minutes.

4. For the icing, beat together the sugar, vanilla and heavy cream. Divide into equal parts, according to the number of colors you are using. For each bowl of icing, add drops of food coloring until you reach the desired depth of color. Put each in a pastry bag (or a plastic bag with the corner cut off) and pipe the icing onto cookies in thin lines. Repeat with each color. Let dry before stacking.

Mildred Clayton, fourth from left, relaxes with her guests. Shirley Darkeh, who contributes authentic African dishes, is at far right.

Cornmeal Pie

MAKES 8 SERVINGS

Mother Tubbs would not part with her recipe for cornmeal pie, so we came up with our own version. It's close, if not quite the same.

½ cup (1 stick) butter, softened
1¼ cups sugar
1 tablespoon yellow cornmeal
½ cup shredded coconut
3 eggs
1 teaspoon vanilla extract
¼ teaspoon salt
1 unbaked 9-inch pie shell

1. Preheat the oven to 350 degrees.
2. Cream together the butter and sugar. Stir in the cornmeal and coconut, mixing thoroughly.
3. Add the eggs, beating in 1 at a time. Mix in the vanilla and salt. Pour the mixture into the pie shell.
4. Bake 30 to 40 minutes, or until a knife inserted in the center comes out clean.

CHAPTER VII

NEW YEAR'S DAY

Menu

Crabmeat Dip
Ruth Knox' Sausage Rolls

———

Osso Buco
Caramelized Onion Mashed Potatoes
Spinach-Cheese Bake
Aunt Vicki's Caesar Salad

———

Roz Sunshine's Apple Crisp
Carrot Cake
Gloria Mueller's Chocolate Fudge Pie
Tiramisu

Good friends welcome

the new year warmly

with fine wine and a hearty lunch

A BRIGHT BEGINNING

At the turning of the year, when daylight is short on Long Island, we all crave warmth and sunshine. In some lucky neighborhoods, there's a house where people congregate as if drawn by a magnet. On Wendy Road in Syosset, that house is one that belongs to the Sunshines, a family that could not be more aptly named.

For a New Year's Day party, they lit a fire in the fireplace, toasted neighbors with wines from Jimmy Sunshine's enviable cellar and spread a buffet of osso buco, mashed potatoes and spinach-cheese bake. Flowers were dramatic.

There's a lesson here: Make the food hearty and plentiful, the wine good and the welcome warm. Don't fuss too much.

Liz and Jimmy make unpretentious party-giving look easy, with a little help from their friends. There's an easy camaraderie on their block, and folks wander in and out of each other's kitchens borrowing a cup of peanut butter here, a roll of paper towels there. The residents of Wendy Road have a name for it: Wendyworld.

Opposite, from left, neighbors Lisa and Nick Mazzillo and Helen and Warren Brand make their way down the buffet line.

That name stands for neighborliness. When Liz was making a cake and her mixer broke down, Ilene Calabretta, a neighbor, lent hers. Liz has a collection of whimsical, one-of-a-kind MacKenzie-Childs plates, but if she doesn't have just the right serving piece for a particular dish, neighbors are happy to lend theirs.

The Sunshines have an easy-going style. When they're not giving parties, they are just as likely to run out to get coffee as to brew it themselves, but Liz is the sort of thoughtful hostess who will transfer the takeout coffee to a thermal pot and keep it warm for a guest.

Whether it's a New Year's buffet for 12 or a summer bash for 100 (complete with a live DJ and three massage therapists to help guests relax), planning ahead is the key.

For this menu, the crab dip was easily prepared ahead, ready to pop in the oven. Sausage rolls, a favorite from Liz' English-born mother, rely on frozen puff pastry. Osso buco and Yukon gold mashed potatoes with caramelized onions were made ahead, and so was the spinach-cheese bake. Only Caesar salad required some last-minute attention.

The lavish spread of desserts was made ahead, too: carrot cake (baked ahead and frozen, then thawed and frosted); apple crisp; fudge pie; the tiramisu, and some luscious chocolate-covered pretzels from a local shop. There was mint chocolate-chip ice cream for the fudge pie, vanilla for the apple crisp — and plenty of whipped cream for everything.

This time, the coffee was served in thin, bone-China teacups, part of a collection that Liz' mother started for her when she was only about 5 years old.

Crabmeat Dip

MAKES ABOUT 8 SERVINGS

The festivities began when partygoers gathered around the fireplace to sip wine and eat dips and sausage rolls before lunch.

½ pound fresh crabmeat, drained
1 (3-ounce) package cream cheese, softened
½ cup mayonnaise
¼ cup minced onion
1 tablespoon lemon juice
⅛ teaspoon hot pepper sauce (such as Tabasco)

Pick over crabmeat and remove any shells. Beat the cream cheese until smooth. Stir in the mayonnaise, onion, crabmeat, lemon juice and hot pepper sauce. Spoon the mixture into a small ovenproof dish. Bake at 350 degrees for 30 minutes or until bubbly. Serve with crackers.

Ruth Knox' Sausage Rolls

MAKES 60 PIECES

Liz Sunshine's mother, Ruth Knox, is the source for these simple but popular hors d'oeuvres.

1 package (2 sheets) frozen puff pastry
3 (12-ounce) packages brown-and-serve sausages
1 egg yolk, beaten

1. Thaw the 2 sheets of pastry according to package instructions. Cut each sheet into 3 long strips.
2. Roll out each strip and cut into 5 equal pieces, each large enough to wrap 1 sausage.
3. Roll the pastry around the sausages, moisten the edges and seal. The sausages will not be entirely enclosed in pastry. Cut each sausage roll in half. Repeat with remaining pastry and sausages. Put on cookie sheets and score the dough twice on top of each roll; do not cut through the sausages.
4. Bake at 375 degrees for about 20 minutes or until light brown. Brush the tops of the sausage rolls with a little beaten egg yolk for the last few minutes of baking. Serve with HP Sauce (available at specialty stores) or mustard.

Osso Buco

MAKES 4 SERVINGS

Newsday adapted this recipe from one Liz Sunshine got from a cooking wares catalog.

8 (2½-inch-thick) veal shank pieces (6 to 8 ounces each)
½ cup flour
2 tablespoons unsalted butter
2 tablespoons olive oil
¼ cup Cognac
½ cup beef broth
1 medium-sized onion, chopped
Salt and freshly ground pepper
Zest of 2 lemons
Rosemary for garnish

1. Coat each veal shank piece evenly with flour, shaking off any excess. Melt the butter with the olive oil over medium-high heat in a large Dutch oven or saute pan with a fitted lid in which the veal pieces will fit in a single layer. Add the veal pieces, cut-side up, and brown on all sides, for about 8 minutes. Remove from heat.
2. In a small pan over medium heat, warm the Cognac. Remove from heat. When away from heat, carefully light the Cognac with a match, and pour the flaming Cognac over the veal pieces. Let the flame go out, and return to low heat.
3. Add the broth, chopped onion, and salt and pepper to taste. Cover and simmer until the veal is tender when pierced with a fork, 1¼ to 2 hours, turning the veal pieces halfway through cooking. When done, transfer the veal to a serving platter. Set aside and cover to keep warm.
4. Remove the pan from the heat and skim off any fat from the surface of the liquid. Return the pan to high heat and boil the liquid until thickened and reduced to about ½ cup. Add salt and pepper to taste. Pour the sauce over the shanks. Grate lemon zest directly onto the veal. Garnish with sprigs of rosemary or other fresh herbs.

Caramelized Onion Mashed Potatoes

MAKES 8 SERVINGS

This is an adaptation of another recipe Liz Sunshine clipped from a catalog.

4 tablespoons unsalted butter
3 tablespoons olive oil
3 small red onions, thinly sliced
4 pounds Yukon Gold potatoes, peeled and quartered
Salt
1½ cups light cream, heated
½ teaspoon white pepper, or to taste

1. In a saute pan over medium-high heat, melt the butter and olive oil. Add the onions and cook until translucent. Reduce the heat to low and let the onions cook until caramelized, about ½ hour. Remove from heat.
2. Put the potatoes in a large pot with enough cold water to cover. Bring to a boil. Add a pinch of salt and boil until tender when pierced with a fork, about 15 minutes. Drain well.
3. Put the potatoes through a ricer or food mill. Slowly add the light cream, stirring constantly, until the potatoes are creamy but not soupy. Mix in the caramelized onions, and add salt and white pepper to taste.

Spinach-Cheese Bake

MAKES 6 TO 8 SERVINGS

3 (10-ounce) packages frozen chopped spinach
3 eggs, beaten
¼ cup flour
1 teaspoon seasoned salt, such as Lawry's
¼ teaspoon ground nutmeg
¼ teaspoon ground black pepper
2 cups creamed cottage cheese
2 cups shredded cheese, 1 cup each of Cheddar and Swiss

1. Cook the spinach according to package instructions. Drain, squeezing out excess moisture.
2. Combine the eggs, flour, seasoned salt, nutmeg and pepper in a bowl. Mix in the cottage cheese, Cheddar cheese, Swiss cheese and spinach.
3. Turn into a buttered 1½-quart casserole and bake at 325 degrees for 50 to 60 minutes.

Aunt Vicki's Caesar Salad

MAKES 8 TO 10 SERVINGS

This family favorite is from Liz Sunshine's sister, Vicki Klem.

½ can anchovies (2 ounces), packed in olive oil
3 large garlic cloves
5 egg yolks (see note)
½ cup freshly grated Parmesan cheese
Lemon juice
6 to 8 ounces olive oil
¼ cup white wine vinegar
2 to 3 large heads of romaine lettuce,
    cleaned and cut in bite-sized pieces

1. Chill all ingredients before making the salad.
2. Puree the anchovies and garlic in a blender. Add the egg yolks, Parmesan cheese, and a few drops of lemon juice. Gradually add the oil while the blender is running. Add vinegar to taste.
3. Toss the dressing with the lettuce.
Note: Use bottled Caesar salad dressing if you don't want to use raw eggs, which may contain salmonella.

Roz Sunshine's Apple Crisp

MAKES 8 SERVINGS

Liz Sunshine likes to give dessert parties, and what better way to welcome the New Year than with a bevy of beautiful desserts. This is her mother-in-law's recipe.

6 large apples (Granny Smiths are good),
    peeled, cored and sliced
Juice of 1 lemon
¾ teaspoon cinnamon
¼ teaspoon nutmeg
1 cup flour
1 cup sugar
½ teaspoon salt
1 teaspoon baking powder
1 egg
⅓ cup melted butter
Vanilla ice cream, for serving

1. Combine the apples, lemon juice, cinnamon and nutmeg and place in an 8-by-8-by-2-inch ungreased pan.
2. In a bowl, combine the flour, sugar, salt, baking powder and egg. Mix until crumbly and spread over the apple mixture. Drizzle the melted butter on top. Bake for 45 minutes at 400 degrees. Serve still warm with vanilla ice cream.

Gloria Mueller's Chocolate Fudge Pie

MAKES 6 TO 8 SERVINGS

Gloria Mueller is an old friend of Liz Sunshine's family, who made this for her when she was a child. This recipe is easily doubled and freezes well. Make one for now, one for later.

2½ squares (2½ ounces) unsweetened chocolate
½ cup (1 stick) butter
1 cup sugar
⅓ cup flour
½ teaspoon salt
1 teaspoon vanilla extract
2 eggs, beaten
Mint ice cream, for serving

1. Preheat the oven to 375 degrees. Butter an 8-inch pie plate.
2. Melt the chocolate and butter over hot water, using a double boiler.
3. Add, in order, the sugar, flour, salt, vanilla and eggs, stirring between each addition. Pour into the prepared pan and bake 20 minutes. (The pie will not look solid when removed from the oven.) Let cool at room temperature for about 2 hours and then refrigerate. Serve with mint ice cream, if desired.

Liz Sunshine, above, serves apple crisp. Jimmy Sunshine, right, and Michael Douglass select wine from the cellar.

Tiramisu

MAKES 8 SERVINGS

Liz Sunshine and a neighbor started Austrian-crystal beading as a hobby that became a business and surprised them by making enough money for a trip to Italy. This recipe for tiramisu was one they picked up on the trip. Unlike many other versions, it can be made without alcohol. If you do not feel confident about the source of your eggs, do not make this recipe, as raw eggs are a must.

4 eggs, separated
4 to 5 tablespoons sugar
¾ to 1 pound mascarpone cheese
About 18 ladyfingers or Italian ladyfingers (savoiardi)
Espresso, port or Marsala
Unsweetened cocoa

1. Mix the egg yolks and sugar together, beating with a mixer until light and airy.
2. Add the mascarpone by hand, folding in. Set aside.
3. Using a mixer, beat the 4 egg whites until peaks form.
4. Fold the egg whites slowly into the yolk mixture.
5. Dip the ladyfingers in espresso (or port or Marsala).
6. Line the bottom of a serving dish, about 8 by 13 inches, with ladyfingers. Add the egg and cheese mixture and refrigerate. When ready to serve, sift unsweetened cocoa on top.

Carrot Cake

MAKES 12 SERVINGS

2 cups sugar
2 cups flour
2 teaspoons cinnamon
2 teaspoons baking soda
1 teaspoon salt
1½ cups corn oil
3 eggs
2 teaspoons vanilla extract
2 cups shredded carrots
1 (8-ounce) can crushed pineapple, drained
1 cup chopped walnuts and pecans, combined
10 ounces shredded sweetened coconut
For frosting:
2 (3-ounce) packages cream cheese, softened
½ cup (1 stick) butter, softened
1 (1-pound) box confectioners' sugar, sifted
Pinch of salt
1 teaspoon vanilla extract

1. Sift together the sugar, flour, cinnamon, baking soda and salt. Add the oil and blend. Add the eggs, 1 at a time, beating after each addition. Add the vanilla. Add the carrots and blend well. Fold in the pineapple, nuts and coconut. Bake at 350 degrees in 2 buttered and floured (9-inch) layer pans for about 40 to 45 minutes. The cake is done when a toothpick inserted into the center comes out with only a few crumbs on it.

2. To make the frosting, blend the cream cheese, butter, sugar, salt and vanilla together until smooth. Frost between the layers and the top and sides of the cake.

Neighbors and friends of Liz and Jimmy Sunshine toast the new year.

CHINESE NEW YEAR

Menu

Diced Chicken in Lettuce Purse
Braised Dried Oysters With Sea Moss (Ho See Faht Choy)
Steamed Whole Fish With Ginger and Scallions
E Mein (Longevity Noodle) With Mushrooms and Chives
Fried Rice, Yangzhou Style

Sweet Red Bean Soup

When the lunar New Year

is celebrated, food takes on

new meanings

A SYMBOLIC BANQUET

Chinese New Year, which falls on the first day of the lunar year — any day from January 10 to February 19 on the Gregorian calendar — is something of a misnomer in the New York area. Jimmy Meng, a prominent Chinese businessman who is also chairman of Queens' Asian-American Coalition, prefers the more inclusive "Lunar New Year" to characterize the holiday, which is celebrated not only by the borough's Chinese residents, but also by Koreans, Indians, Pakistanis, Bangladeshis, Thais and Filipinos, among others whose traditional calendar is lunar.

Of course, many lunar New Year's traditions are singularly Chinese. And to usher in 4698, the Year of the Dragon, Jimmy and his family gathered at Full Ho Seafood Restaurant in Flushing for a quintessentially Chinese New Year's banquet. The menu tied the feast to the culinary traditions of Hong Kong (home of the restaurant's chef, King-Pui Hui) and Taiwan (Jimmy's birthplace), and the meal was freighted with Chinese symbolism; surfacing again and again were the color red

Shark's fin soup is ladled into individual bowls.

for happiness, gold for wealth, round shapes signifying completeness and perfection.

Seated at a round, red-clothed table, the family — Jimmy and his wife, Shiao-mei, his parents and mother-in-law, two of the Mengs' three children and three of their nieces and nephews — kicked off the meal with a roast suckling pig whose golden skin shimmered. Shark's fin soup, a test of any Chinese kitchen's skill, followed. Next came a traditional New Year's dish of minced squab served in lettuce leaves that had been meticulously trimmed so that each one was round. Meng explained that "with the squab and vegetables all chopped and mixed together, the dish means harmony. And after we eat it, there is no misunderstanding." The next dish, abalone with shiitake mushrooms, is a specialty of both chef Hui and his brother, who is a chef in Hong Kong.

Dish number five, de rigeur at New Year's, consisted of dried scallops and oysters atop a bed of "black moss," a hair-like seaweed. The transliteration of its name, *ho see faht choy*, is a play on words. "Ho see" means both oyster and good business; "faht choy" are the long strands of seaweed that, fittingly, symbolize long life. Hence the dish's name can be translated as "good business, long life." Likewise, a chicken dish is always served at New Year's because the Chinese character for chicken is the same as for "lucky." This night, the chicken, dish six, caused an audible gasp when it was placed on the table, so beautifully was the bird presented.

Shark's Fin Soup

There's no greater test of a Chinese banquet chef's skill than shark's fin soup. George Chuang, proprietor of Full Ho Seafood Restaurant in Flushing, explained that it is the fin itself that distinguishes a run-of-the-mill soup from a definitive one. The most valuable portion of the shark's dorsal fin is the wide part at its base and it is this cut of fin — to the tune of $380 a pound — that Full Ho uses. The broth, made from chicken, beef, scallops, shrimp and mushrooms, simmers for close to 10 hours, resulting in a broth that is both rich and clear. Lesser soups, said Chuang, might be made from a thinner broth that had been thickened with cornstarch. Chef King-Pui Hui added that the shark's fin itself, for all its expense, doesn't have a particularly pleasing flavor or texture. That's why, he explained, it requires such laborious doctoring.

"From south to north, east to west, you can always find lobster and scallop on a banquet menu," Meng said of the seventh dish, the significance of which he summed up succinctly: "Lobster costs a lot of money, scallops are round." The last of the main dishes was fish. Meng explained that at home-based New Year's banquets, the fish is prepared and brought to the table but not eaten, because a whole fish symbolizes surplus and this meaning is amplified if the fish is saved until the next day. At the restaurant, however, tradition was modified. "If we left it here," noted Meng, "the restaurant staff would just eat it."

Rice is central to any Chinese meal. The fried rice that constituted the banquet's ninth dish, however, presented a paradox. Full Ho's proprietor George Chuang explained that his chef makes some of the best fried rice to be found in New York, but as good as it was, the Meng party did not finish it. Meng explained that it's disrespectful to the host to finish the rice at the end of a banquet because it implies that you're not completely stuffed. Not to mention that being stuffed would prevent you from eating the tenth and final course, another New Year's must-eat: stir-fried noodles.

Three desserts later, when the meal was over, Jimmy's father, Wei Feng Meng, pulled his chair away from the table and prepared to distribute red envelopes to his grandchildren. It's a tradition on New Year's for children to receive *hong bao*, red envelopes full of money, from their elders.

While the children lined up dutifully to receive their gifts, Jimmy reflected on the Year of the Dragon and what it promised. "The dragon means power and energy," he said, adding that this year he planned to put his energy into Queens' pan-Asian community. All of the groups that follow the lunar calendar would be participating in the parade formerly known as The Chinese New Year Parade — now billed as Flushing's Lunar New Year Parade. Jimmy prefers the new name. He said, "It's about harmony."

About the recipes: The food that comes out of a Chinese restaurant kitchen, cooked by a professional chef with access to rare ingredients and blisteringly hot woks, can't be easily duplicated in most people's homes. To adapt the dishes served at Full Ho Seafood Restaurant's New Year's banquet, we turned to Norman Weinstein, an instructor at Peter Kump's New York Cooking School and a noted Chinese cooking teacher. Weinstein attended the banquet and created these recipes based on conversations with the restaurant staff and his own research. For instance, in the first dish, Weinstein substituted dark-meat chicken for the squab used in Full Ho's version.

Diced Chicken in Lettuce Purse

MAKES 4 TO 6 SERVINGS

1 pound boneless chicken thighs, finely diced
2 tablespoons soy sauce, divided
2 tablespoons dry sherry, divided
1 egg white
4 tablespoons cornstarch, divided
2 tablespoons vegetable oil
¾ cup chicken broth
1 tablespoon oyster sauce
Freshly ground black pepper to taste
1 to 2 whole iceberg lettuce leaves for each person
3 cups vegetable or corn oil
1 Chinese pork sausage (lahp cheung), finely diced
¼ cup dry-roasted peanuts, lightly crushed
¼ cup finely diced scallion, white and green parts
1 tablespoon finely minced fresh ginger
1 tablespoon Asian sesame oil

1. Combine the diced chicken with 1 tablespoon of the soy sauce and 1 tablespoon of the sherry. Mix well. Add the egg white. Mix again. Add half of the cornstarch and the 2 tablespoons of vegetable oil and mix again. Refrigerate at least ½ hour. Bring to room temperature before cooking.

2. Combine the chicken broth, the remaining soy sauce and sherry, oyster sauce and pepper. Set aside. Separate the lettuce leaves and place on a serving platter.

3. Heat a wok until vapors appear. Add the oil; heat to 225 degrees. Add the diced chicken and stir with chopsticks or a ladle to separate. Poach for about 20 seconds. Drain the oil through a colander into a heat-proof bowl and set the chicken aside.

4. Return 2 tablespoons of the drained oil to the wok. Heat for 10 seconds. Add the sausage, peanuts, scallion and ginger. Stir 10 to 15 seconds to heat through. Add the chicken and cook for another 15 to 20 seconds. Remove to a platter.

5. Mix the remaining cornstarch with ¼ cup cold water. Add the reserved broth mixture to the wok. When nearly at the boil, stir in enough of the cornstarch mixture to thicken the broth to the consistency of a light syrup. Add the chicken and sesame oil. Stir to mix well. Place the mixture in the lettuce leaves on the serving platter.

Braised Dried Oysters With Sea Moss (Ho See Faht Choy)

MAKES 4 TO 6 SERVINGS

This recipe presents a simplified version of a very complicated procedure. Weinstein consulted not only with Full Ho owner George Chuang, but also owners Danny Tsoi and Jimmy Cheng of Ocean Palace in Brooklyn. Select 1½-inch-sized dried oysters that still have a little give to them, and the thick gray-white mushrooms (bahk goo) rather than the brown ones. Neither ingredient is cheap. This dish can be made a day ahead. Reheat by steaming it for 10 to 12 minutes.

12 dried oysters (ho see)
1½ cups chicken broth
10 (¼-inch-thick) coins fresh ginger
Whites of 3 scallions, lightly crushed
3 tablespoons dry sherry
1 tablespoon oyster sauce
1 teaspoon sugar
12 thick, dried Chinese mushrooms (bahk goo)
1 (1-ounce) package black sea moss (faht choy)
3 cups shredded lettuce
3 tablespoons vegetable oil
2 tablespoons cornstarch

1. Soak the oysters in hot water for 3 to 4 hours. Rinse, place in a saucepan with the chicken broth, ginger, scallions, sherry, oyster sauce and sugar. Bring to barely a simmer, cover and cook for 1 hour.

2. Soak the mushrooms in hot water for 30 minutes or until soft. Drain, remove and discard the stems. Add to the oysters for the last 30 minutes they cook.

3. Soak half a handful of the black moss in hot water for 15 to 20 minutes. Drain and rinse under cold water. Reserve.

4. When ready to prepare the dish, stir-fry the lettuce in the oil until wilted. Place in a 9-inch pie plate. Remove the oysters and mushrooms from the broth with a slotted spoon, reserving the broth. Neatly mound the oysters in the center of the plate. Place the mushrooms around the perimeter.

5. Place the soaked moss in a bowl and pour the broth over it. Remove and discard the ginger and scallions. Let stand 2 to 3 minutes. Place a strainer over the saucepan and pour in soaking moss. Remove the moss from the strainer and place it in the serving plate between the oysters and the mushrooms.

6. Bring the strained broth to a near-boil. Combine the cornstarch with 3 tablespoons cold water. Add enough to thicken the broth to the consistency of a light syrup. Ladle over the mushrooms, moss and oysters on the serving plate.

Steamed Whole Fish
With Ginger and Scallions

MAKES 4 TO 6 SERVINGS

To steam a 1½- to 2-pound fish, you will need a good sized roasting pan with a cover, two inverted tuna-fish cans with tops and bottoms removed, a large heat-proof platter and a Chinese plate lifter.

1 sea bass or any firm-fleshed fish, about 1½ to 2 pounds, cleaned and scaled with head and tail left on
½ teaspoon salt
2 tablespoons rice wine or dry sherry
¼ cup vegetable oil
½ cup finely shredded fresh ginger
2 to 3 scallions, white and green parts, sliced into thin shreds on a deep diagonal
¼ cup high-quality thin soy sauce

1. Rinse and dry the fish thoroughly. Make vertical slashes to the bone, 1½ inches apart, from the tail to the head on 1 side only. Place the fish, cut-side up, on a platter. Sprinkle with salt and wine. Let stand 5 minutes.

2. Add 1½ inches water to the roasting pan and place the cans in the center, about 4 to 5 inches apart. Over high heat, bring the water to a boil on the stovetop across two burners. Place the platter with the fish on top of the cans, cover the roasting pan, and cook over rapidly boiling water for 8 to 10 minutes. A 2-pound fish will take 10 minutes.

3. The last minute or so while the fish is steaming, heat the vegetable oil in a skillet until it is smoking. Add the ginger and reduce the heat so the oil stays hot but the ginger doesn't burn.

4. Remove the platter from the roasting pan, drain all the liquid and place on another platter to facilitate carrying. Top the fish with the shredded scallions.

5. Remove the hot oil from the heat, add the soy sauce, and pour over the fish. To serve, spoon off meat in sections, using the slits as a guide, working from tail to head. When the top sections have been served, lift the center bone from the tail to head, remove, and serve the bottom half.

Activity swirls in the kitchen of Full Ho Seafood Restaurant while a roast suckling pig awaits its big moment.

E Mein (Longevity Noodle) With Mushrooms and Chives

MAKES 4 TO 6 SERVINGS

The white sauce for this dish can be prepared days in advance. The noodle package may say "prepared," "steamed" or "cooked" noodles.

For the white sauce:
2 cups chicken broth, 5 tablespoons reserved
1 tablespoon dry sherry
1 teaspoon sugar (optional)
1 teaspoon kosher salt or to taste
5 to 6 (½-inch) chunks fresh ginger
4 cloves garlic, peeled
Whites of 5 scallions, smashed
For the noodles:
6 dried Chinese mushrooms
1 bunch Chinese green or yellow chives
5 cups vegetable oil
1 (16-ounce) package steamed noodles
3 tablespoons cornstarch
Greens of 5 to 6 scallions, minced

1. To make the white sauce, place the chicken broth (except the 5 reserved tablespoons) in a saucepan. Bring to a simmer. Add the sherry, sugar, salt, ginger, garlic and scallions. Simmer for 15 minutes. Strain out the solids, discard, and reserve the white sauce.

2. To make the noodles, cover the mushrooms with hot water and soak for 30 to 40 minutes or until soft. Remove and discard stems. Mince the caps and set aside. Remove the tough ends from the chives and discard. Cut the chives into 4- to 5-inch sections.

3. Heat the 5 cups oil in a wok or skillet to 365 degrees. Add the noodles to the hot oil. When they are lightly browned, remove with a large strainer. Drain and set aside. This step may be done in advance. Drain the oil from the wok and reserve 3 tablespoons. Combine the cornstarch and 5 tablespoons of reserved broth.

4. Return the 3 tablespoons of the reserved oil to the wok. Heat 10 seconds. Add the chives and scallions. Stir 15 seconds. Add the mushrooms and the white sauce. Bring to a simmer. Thicken lightly with the cornstarch mixture. Add the noodles. Stir until all the broth has been absorbed. Place in a bowl and serve immediately.

**Above left, Mei-Hsien Wang holds a pork-stuffed pancake.
Left, Full Ho's banquet chicken, which is boned, skinned, minced and reconstituted.**

Fried Rice, Yangzhou Style

MAKES 6 TO 8 SERVINGS

"Dry-frying" rice (frying without oil) the way Full Ho does requires much more heat than most domestic stoves can produce, so this recipe calls for oil. Full Ho's fried rice is also very spare — calling for egg whites, lobster and Chinese broccoli — but here Norman Weinstein has created a more traditional recipe that uses whole eggs, roast pork and shrimp as well.

4 cups cold cooked white rice
½ pound small shrimp, peeled but not deveined
6 fresh water chestnuts
3 stalks Chinese broccoli (discard leaves)
1 cup diced roast pork
½ cup diced scallion greens
½ to 1 cup vegetable oil, divided
3 eggs, beaten with a pinch of salt
1 cup diced lobster meat (optional)
Salt and pepper to taste

1. Moisten your hands with cold water. Gently separate the grains of rice into a bowl. Reserve. Cut the shrimp in half (or, if very small, leave whole). Peel and dice the water chestnuts. Blanch the broccoli stalks for 3 minutes. Refresh in cold water, split lengthwise into quarters, and then dice. Combine the water chestnuts and broccoli with the roast pork and diced scallions.

2. Heat a wok or skillet until vapor appears. Add 2 to 3 tablespoons of the oil. Heat 10 seconds, swirl the pan, and add the eggs. Stir with a spatula until the eggs are semi-firm. Break up into small pieces. Remove to a large plate.

3. Add a few more tablespoons of oil to the wok. Heat 10 seconds. Add half the shrimp. Stir-fry over high heat 20 to 30 seconds. Remove to a plate. Cook the remaining shrimp and remove to the plate. Stir-fry the diced lobster in 3 batches. Place on the plate.

4. Glaze the wok with oil. Add the rice ½ cup at a time, tossing constantly to heat through. Add salt and pepper to taste. Add the eggs, shrimp, lobster, roast pork, scallions, broccoli and water chestnuts. Season to taste with salt and pepper. Toss gently to distribute the ingredients evenly and heat through. Place on a serving platter and serve in rice bowls.

Andy Meng receives his New Year's gift. Opposite, at the banquet's finale, Shiao-mei Meng takes some fruit. Her husband, Jimmy Meng, is at left.

Sweet Red Bean Soup

MAKES 8 TO 12 SERVINGS

This is a traditional Chinese dessert often found at a banquet table.

1 (14-ounce) package (2 cups) small red beans
18 pitted red dates
18 dried lotus seeds
3 to 4 pieces dried tangerine peel
1 (2-inch) chunk yellow rock sugar or ⅓ cup granulated sugar

Pick through the beans to discard any stones. Rinse several times. Place in a 4- to 5-quart heavy pot with 8 cups water. Bring to a boil, then cover and simmer for 1 hour. Add the dates, lotus seeds and dried tangerine peel. Simmer, covered, another 30 minutes. Add the sugar and simmer, covered, another 30 minutes, or until the beans are soft and the soup has thickened. You may remove the tangerine peel, if desired, although it is often left in. Serve in bowls. (Recipe can be halved.)

Note: If you want soup with a little more body, puree ½ to ¾ cup of the beans and liquid and return to the pot.

CHAPTER IX

PASSOVER

Menu

———

Gloria's Chicken Soup
Matzoh Balls

———

Haroset
Brisket
Passover Chicken
Matzoh Farfel Kugel

———

Mock Oatmeal Cookies

A Great Neck family

adapts the seder

for modern times

AN ENDURING RITUAL

Passover, more than any other Jewish holiday, is about food. The week-long observance begins with a ritual cleaning of the kitchen, ridding it of all traces of *hametz*, or forbidden leavened bread products. The seder is the ceremonial meal that is part of the retelling of the story of Passover, the story of the flight of the Jews from Egypt.

Although Jewish people observe the holiday with varying degrees of formality and strict adherence to ancient laws, they all share a pleasure in the ritual. Passover links the past with the future with the telling of an old story to the youngest members of the family.

At the Great Neck home of Jerry and Gloria Landsberg, the Passover seder is part religious ceremony, part feast and part pageant. The couple draws big crowds — routinely more than 24 guests on each of two nights — largely due to their ability to constantly adapt this ancient holiday to their modern, changing family and lifestyle.

Gloria started making seders more than 30 years ago, as a young mother of four. Now she is the grandmother

Melissa Seltzer, at left, next to her sister Alison, who nibbles on a piece of matzoh.

of many and she continues to welcome more family additions to the table. It's no big deal for the unflappable Gloria. "Once you're cooking you just keep cooking. I serve the same menu each night," she said, referring to her seder staples, which include a savory dish of chicken with raisins, a beloved peach kugel and, for dessert, delicious mock oatmeal cookies. "After the first night, I wash the dishes and put them right back on the table for the next night. I just switch from one color tablecloth to another color."

Jerry leads the service, adapting his program to suit his audience. Years ago, when his old college friend, a Methodist minister, came for Passover with his family, Jerry was careful to include a more detailed account of the Exodus. But as young grandchildren have been added, Jerry has at times cut some of the narrative to hold their attention. When a granddaughter recently decided the family wasn't singing enough, he added more songs. These days, with most of the children at the seder under the age of 7, the best strategy seems to be speed-reading the Haggadah. Said Jerry, "I've made into an Evelyn Wood-type service.

"I realize there is an aspect of solemnity to the occasion," he said. "But we want to make it enjoyable for everyone. Of all the holidays, this is the most fun."

Homemade Gefilte Fish

Gefilte fish is much easier to make at home than you might expect, especially if your fishmonger grinds the the fish and onion for you. In addition to white fish, pike and carp are traditionally used during Passover. One note: Unlike other types of stock, fish stock doesn't get better the more it's cooked; any longer than 30 minutes, it becomes bitter.

Fish Stock
Fish frames (obtained from fishmonger)
1 onion, sliced
2 stalks celery, sliced
3 teaspoons salt
2 teaspoons sugar
7 peppercorns

Place ingredients in stockpot and cover with 12 cups cold water. Bring to a boil, reduce heat and simmer 30 minutes. Strain, and discard fish frames and vegetables.

Fish Balls
1½ pounds white fish
1 pound pike
½ pound carp
1 onion
2 eggs
2 teaspoons sugar
½ cup matzoh meal
½ teaspoon ground white pepper
To add to stock:
3 carrots, peeled and sliced
1 teaspoon sugar

1. Unless your fishmonger has done it for you, cut fish and onion into pieces and place in bowl of a food processor and finely chop, being careful to not over process. Place fish and onion in bowl and blend in eggs, sugar, matzoh meal and white pepper. Cover and refrigerate ½ hour.
2. Add carrots and sugar to stock and bring to a boil. With wet hands, shape ½ cup fish mixture into an oval. Repeat with remaining fish. Place ovals into stock, making sure all the fish balls are covered (add water if necessary). Cook over medium heat for up to 1½ hours.
3. Remove fish balls and carrots and refrigerate. Boil stock to reduce it to 6 cups, cool and then add to fish. Refrigerate and serve cold with horseradish. Makes 25 fish balls.

Gloria's Chicken Soup

MAKES 10 TO 12 SERVINGS

Gloria Landsberg makes all her soups in the oven, cooking them on low heat for several hours. If you don't make this soup overnight, cook the chickens for 8 hours, or, as Landsberg said, until the kitchen smells delicious.

2 (3-pound) chickens
1 onion, peeled and quartered
2 carrots, peeled and cut into 2-inch pieces
2 ribs celery, cut into thirds
Salt and pepper to taste

1. Remove neck and giblets and rinse. Place both chickens in a large ovenproof pot (4 gallons or more). Cover with hot tap water.
2. Put the pot in the oven and turn the oven on to 400 degrees. When the water begins to boil, lower the temperature to 250 degrees and go to sleep.
3. In the morning, take the pot out of the oven. Remove the chickens from the liquid and reserve them for another use. Add the onion, carrots and celery to the stock and continue to cook for 5 to 6 more hours. Remove from the oven, strain and discard the vegetables. Season to taste with salt and pepper.

Matzoh Balls

MAKES 18 TO 20 PIECES

Matzoh balls expand as they cook. These will be about 2 inches in diameter.

4 tablespoons schmaltz, at room temperature
4 eggs, lightly beaten
1 cup matzoh meal
1½ teaspoons salt
4 tablespoons chicken stock, or water
7 chicken bouillon cubes

1. In a medium bowl, mix the schmaltz (chicken fat) and eggs. Add the matzoh meal and salt. Mix well. Add the chicken stock. Mix with a fork until the ingredients are well blended. Cover and refrigerate for at least 2 hours.
2. Fill a 4-quart pot with water and add the bouillon cubes. Bring to a boil over high heat. As soon as the water boils, wet your hands and shape the dough into golf-ball-size balls. Drop the matzoh balls into the boiling water 1 at a time.
3. When the balls rise to the surface, cover the pot and reduce the heat. Continue to simmer until the balls sink to the bottom of the pot, about 45 minutes. Remove with a slotted spoon to a plate to cool. Reheat in the chicken soup before serving.

Haroset

MAKES 20 SERVINGS

This recipe for haroset comes from Gloria's family cookbook. It originally made twice as much, because her extended family is quite large.

6 apples, preferably Gala or Winesap
3 tablespoons honey
1 teaspoon cinnamon
Juice of 1 lemon
1 cup slivered or chopped almonds, preferably toasted
1 cup chopped pecans
4 tablespoons sweet kosher wine

Core all the apples and peel 3 of them. Cut into quarters. Place all the apples in the bowl of a food processor and pulse until the apples are chopped (be careful not to puree them). In a large bowl, combine the apples with the remaining ingredients. Taste, and add more cinnamon or wine, if needed.

Gloria Landsberg lights a candle as her husband Jerry reads the Passover story.

Brisket

MAKES 10 TO 12 SERVINGS

One nearly universal ingredient in Passover brisket (aside from the brisket) is packaged onion soup mix. We added some vegetables and seasonings to Gloria's recipe for extra color and depth of flavor.

1 package dried onion soup mix
4 onions, halved and thinly sliced
½ cup celery (2 ribs), with some leaves, chopped
¾ cup carrots (about 3 carrots), peeled and
    cut into ½-inch rounds
1 cup ketchup
1 cup dry red wine
1 (4- to 5-pound) beef brisket

1. Lay a sheet of heavy-duty aluminum foil in a 9-by-13-inch pan or a casserole large enough to hold the meat. Combine all the ingredients except the beef and spread the mixture on the foil. Place the brisket on top of the mixture, fat side up, spooning some of the sauce on top.

2. Cover the meat tightly with heavy-duty aluminum foil, sealing the edges, and bake at 350 degrees for 4 hours, or until the meat is fork-tender.

Passover Chicken

MAKES 10 SERVINGS

2 tablespoons vegetable oil
3 pounds boneless, skinless chicken pieces
2 sweet onions, chopped
Salt and pepper to taste
1½ tablespoons tomato paste
¼ cup raisins
Juice of 1 lemon
1 teaspoon sugar

1. In a large skillet or Dutch oven, heat the oil over medium-high heat and brown the chicken. Remove.
2. In the same pan, saute the onions over medium heat until golden.
3. Return the thigh pieces to the pan and sprinkle with salt and pepper. Dissolve the tomato paste in 1½ cups water and add to the pan along with the raisins. Cover, reduce the heat and simmer for 10 minutes. Add the breast pieces and cook another 15 minutes.
4. Remove chicken to a serving platter. Add the lemon juice and sugar to the pot and stir until the sugar is dissolved. Pour some of the juices over the chicken and pass the rest separately when serving.

Matzoh Farfel Kugel

MAKES 16 SERVINGS

Gloria said, "If you give your readers only one recipe for Passover, make it this one." We agree.

1 (29-ounce) can sliced peaches
1 (15-ounce) can sliced peaches
7 eggs
½ cup sugar
1 teaspoon vanilla extract
1 teaspoon salt
1½ cups (3 sticks) margarine, melted and cooled
1 pound matzoh farfel
1 tablespoon sugar
½ teaspoon cinnamon

1. Drain the peaches, reserving 1½ cups of the liquid.
2. Beat the eggs. Mixing between each addition, add the sugar, vanilla, salt, peach liquid, melted margarine and matzoh farfel.
3. Pour half the mixture into a 9-by-13-inch baking pan. Arrange half the peaches on top. Cover with the remaining mixture. Arrange the remaining peaches on top. Sprinkle the cinnamon and sugar on top.
4. Place on a foil-lined cookie sheet to catch drips. Bake 1 hour at 350 degrees or until set and browned.

Easy Tsimmes

When Jewish people say, "Don't make a tsimmes out of it," that means don't make a big fuss. But making tsimmes is pretty simple. The dish is made of root vegetables, usually carrots and potatoes, sweetened with sugar or honey. It can be served as an appetizer, main course or a side dish. A favorite for Rosh Hashanah because it symbolizes the hopes of sweetness for the New Year, it works well for Passover, too.

Sweet Potato Tsimmes
3 pounds sweet potatoes (about 5 medium),
    peeled and diced
1 pound carrots, peeled and cut into 1-inch slices
½ cup pitted prunes, halved
1 cup orange juice
¼ cup brown sugar
1 (20-ounce) can pears, drained and
    cut into 1-inch chunks
1 (11-ounce) can mandarin oranges, drained
2 tablespoons margarine

Boil sweet potatoes and carrots until tender, about 20 minutes. Drain and mash. Fold in prunes. In bowl, combine orange juice and brown sugar. Place potato mixture into greased 6-quart casserole. Top with juice. Cover with foil and bake 30 minutes in 350-degree oven. Remove foil and fold in pears and mandarin oranges, dot top with margarine and bake uncovered 15 minutes or until fruit is warmed through. Makes 6 servings.

Mock Oatmeal Cookies

MAKES 4 TO 5 DOZEN

When you taste these cookies, it is difficult to believe they were made without oatmeal.

⅔ cup vegetable oil
1½ cups sugar
4 eggs
1 teaspoon vanilla extract
1 teaspoon cinnamon
2 cups matzoh meal
2 cups matzoh farfel
1 cup raisins

Preheat the oven to 350 degrees. Combine all the ingredients in a mixing bowl. Drop by tablespoonfuls onto a well-greased cookie sheet, leaving 2 inches in between. Bake for 18 to 20 minutes. Remove immediately to cooling racks.

The Passover Haggadah

EASTER

Menu

Salmon Quiche
Roast Leg of Lamb With Potatoes
Asparagus With Hollandaise Sauce
Puree of Turnips and Parsnips With Shallots

Tipsy Cake (Trifle)
Bread and Butter Pudding
Irish Coffee

A SPRING BRUNCH

Irish roots are revisited with a buffet of seasonal foods

On Easter, Christians celebrate the central article of their faith: the resurrection of Jesus Christ. Because the holiday is a movable feast that usually coincides with the season's first daffodils and dogwood blossoms, it is also bound to the age-old and universal idea of spring. The themes of fertility and rebirth are evident in the Easter traditions of eggs and bunnies, and, of course, in the foods that grace the Easter table.

The Roughan family of Southampton wouldn't think of celebrating Easter without a traditional roast lamb or without the eggs that show up in virtually every course of their meal: the salmon quiche, the hollandaise sauce that naps asparagus, and the custards at the heart of both desserts, trifle and bread pudding.

Then there are the roast potatoes. Root vegetables are not all that evocative of spring, but Joe and Noreen Roughan hail from Limerick, Ireland, and they are not about to entertain the extended brood — five children, their spouses and, at last count, eight grandchildren — without potatoes, not to mention the parsnip-turnip

Joe and Noreen Roughan's grandchildren gather Easter eggs. From left, Keri Christensen, and Thomas and Aidan Roughan.

puree that always makes an appearance.

The Roughans' grown kids tend to congregate in the kitchen of the ranch-style house in Southampton and talk about growing up in Rockville Centre, where their mother Noreen would dress them up in brand-new Easter finery before shepherding them off to St. Agnes' for mass. The meal afterwards was a grand sit-down affair complete with candles and the good table linens. Now, the number of grandchildren necessitates a more freewheeling buffet brunch, with family members seating themselves in the eat-in kitchen, dining room or living room.

While the Roughans' children reminisce about Easters in Nassau County, their parents remember Easter back in County Limerick. "It was much more religious when we were growing up," Noreen recalled. "On Holy Thursday, all the churches had the Blessed Sacrament on display. You'd go from one church to the other and kneel down and pray. Good Friday you'd go to church and do the Fourteen Stations. Saturday, church was closed, but then on Sunday, well, Easter Sunday was such a festive time. The mass symbolized a new beginning, and it was springtime."

For All Those Eggs

An Easter celebration with children usually includes decorating eggs and, consequently, results in a large quantity of hard-cooked ones. If you're tired of egg salad, consider making deviled eggs.

Deviled Eggs

12 hard-cooked eggs
½ cup mayonnaise
1 to 2 tablespoons Dijon mustard
4 tablespoons finely minced parsley, chives, chervil or a combination, divided
Salt and pepper to taste

Peel the eggs and halve lengthwise. Scoop the yolks into a bowl and combine with the mayonnaise, mustard and 3 tablespoons of the minced herbs. Add salt and pepper to taste. Spoon the mixture back into the whites and sprinkle with the remaining herbs.

From top: Sean Roughan with Ed Brady and his son, Eamon.

Salmon Quiche

MAKES 6 SERVINGS

The ideal pan for this quiche is an 8-by-11-inch rectangular removable-bottom tart pan. A 9-inch round tart pan or shallow pie plate will work as well.

½ (1-pound, 1-ounce) package frozen puff pastry
1 small onion, minced
2 tablespoons butter
2 eggs
½ cup milk
Salt and pepper to taste
6 ounces fresh salmon, poached
1 tablespoon chopped fresh dill, plus sprigs for garnish

1. Thaw the pastry until it is pliable. Roll it out to fit the pan and trim it, leaving a 1-inch overhang. Fold the edge over on itself and crimp with a fork. Freeze for 1 hour, then place a sheet of foil over the dough, pour in dry beans or pie weights and bake in a preheated, 350-degree oven for 8 to 10 minutes. The pastry should not color.
2. Saute the onion in the butter until soft and set aside. Beat the eggs lightly and add the milk, salt and pepper.
3. Flake the salmon over the baked dough. Sprinkle on the onion and chopped dill. Pour in the egg mixture and bake 30 to 40 minutes. Garnish with sprigs of dill.

Roast Leg of Lamb With Potatoes

MAKES 8 TO 12 SERVINGS

1 (8-pound) whole leg of lamb
6 cloves garlic, peeled
2 to 3 sprigs rosemary, plus more for garnish
⅓ cup Dijon mustard
¼ cup olive oil, divided
Salt and pepper to taste
3 pounds red new potatoes or Yukon Golds

1. With a sharp knife, make slits all over the lamb. Sliver the garlic and cut the needles from the rosemary sprigs. Stuff the garlic and needles into the slits.
2. Combine the mustard, 1 tablespoon of oil, salt and pepper, and smear over lamb. Let sit up to 2 hours at room temperature.
3. Preheat the oven to 350 degrees. Cut the potatoes into large chunks. In a large roasting pan, combine the potatoes with the remaining oil, salt and pepper. Place the lamb on a rack in the pan. Roast until an instant-read thermometer inserted in the center reads 125 degrees for rare, checking after 1½ hours. Remove the lamb from the oven, cover it with foil and let it rest for 20 minutes before carving. The meat will continue to cook. Continue cooking the potatoes if they are not yet nicely browned.

Asparagus With Hollandaise Sauce

MAKES 12 SERVINGS

Asparagus captures the very essence of spring.

1½ cups (3 sticks) unsalted butter
6 tablespoons water
6 egg yolks
Salt and white pepper to taste
Juice of 1 lemon
3 pounds asparagus, trimmed and steamed until just tender

1. Melt the butter in a saucepan or in the microwave in a measuring cup. Skim off the foam and let the butter cool until tepid.
2. In a small, heavy saucepan, whisk the water and egg yolks with salt and pepper for 30 seconds until totally integrated. Set the pan over very low heat and whisk for 3 minutes, or until the mixture leaves a ribbon trail for 5 seconds. Make sure the pan doesn't get too hot because the yolks will cook.
3. Remove from the heat and whisk in the butter 1 tablespoon at a time, until the sauce thickens, then add the remaining butter in a steady stream. Don't pour in the milky residue from the bottom of the butter. Stir in the lemon juice and season. If the sauce is too thick, add more lemon juice or water. Place the asparagus on a platter and top with the sauce.

Puree of Turnips and Parsnips With Shallots

MAKES 12 SERVINGS

Folks who claim they don't like turnips or parsnips probably will like this.

5 pounds parsnips, peeled and cut into chunks
1 pound turnips, peeled and cut into chunks
Salt and pepper to taste
½ to ¾ cup (1 to 1½ sticks) butter, divided
6 large shallots, thinly sliced
½ teaspoon grated nutmeg
½ cup chopped parsley

1. Place the parsnips and turnips in a saucepan with water to cover. Add salt. Bring to a simmer and cook until the vegetables are tender, 30 to 40 minutes.
2. Heat 4 tablespoons of the butter in a skillet over high heat. Saute the shallots until golden, then remove and drain.
3. Drain parsnips and turnips, reserving a small amount of the cooking liquid. Puree the parsnips and turnips in the bowl of a food processor with as much of the remaining butter as you like, adding a little of the reserved cooking liquid to thin if necessary. Season with nutmeg, salt and pepper. Turn the vegetables into a serving dish and top with the fried shallots and parsley.

Making Irish Coffee

Joe Roughan, whose father taught him how to make Irish coffee back in Ireland, always presides over this end-of-meal ritual. According to him, the right ingredients aren't enough, there's the technique. "You see some people stir Irish coffee. You don't stir it. You're supposed to drink the coffee through the cream."

Joe Roughan's Irish Coffee

⅓ to ½ cup Irish whiskey
1 tablespoon plus 1 teaspoon sugar, divided
½ cup whipping cream
4 cups freshly brewed coffee

1. In a pitcher, combine the whiskey with 1 tablespoon sugar and stir. Let stand until the sugar is completely dissolved.
2. Whip the cream with remaining teaspoon of sugar just until beater leaves marks on surface of cream. Set aside.
3. Pour whiskey-sugar mixture into each of 4 stemmed glasses. Stick a metal spoon into each glass as you fill it with hot coffee. Finally, pour the cream into the glass, breaking its fall over the back of a tablespoon. Do not stir. Makes 4 servings.

At left, Keri Christensen holds her 3-month-old brother, William. Above, Joe Roughan tops off the Irish coffee with cream and then Patty Corace, Patty Christensen and Laura Roughan enjoy mugs of it.

Tipsy Cake (Trifle)

MAKES 12 SERVINGS

This recipe is flexible and can accommodate any stray nuts or fruit.

2 (3-ounce) packages vanilla pudding/pie filling mix
4 cups milk
3 (3-ounce) packages ladyfingers
⅓ cup raspberry jam
¼ cup Triple Sec or Cointreau
¼ cup dry sherry
12 amaretti (almond cookies), crushed
2 cups whipping cream
2 tablespoons confectioners' sugar
½ teaspoon vanilla extract
½ cup slivered almonds, toasted
½ cup fresh raspberries

1. Prepare both packages of pudding mix according to package instructions, using the 4 cups of milk. Cover with plastic wrap so a skin doesn't form, and refrigerate.
2. Split the ladyfingers lengthwise. Stand them upright around the inside of a 2- to 3-quart trifle bowl. Make sandwiches of the remaining ladyfingers, using the jam as filling; arrange half of them in the bottom of the bowl.
3. In a small bowl, combine the liqueur and sherry; sprinkle half over the ladyfingers in the trifle bowl. Spread half of the cooled pudding over the ladyfingers, then sprinkle with half the crushed cookies. Repeat layers.
4. In a chilled bowl, whip the cream, confectioners' sugar and vanilla until stiff peaks form. Spread over the top of the trifle. Refrigerate, covered, several hours. Garnish with the nuts and berries.

Bread and Butter Pudding

MAKES 12 SERVINGS

This simple recipe is a Roughan-family favorite.

8 to 10 slices white sandwich bread
Butter
½ cup sugar
2 teaspoons cinnamon
1 cup golden raisins
4 cups milk
4 eggs

Preheat the oven to 350 degrees. Remove the crusts from the bread. Butter the bread and cut into triangles. Combine the sugar and cinnamon. Grease a 6- to 8-cup ovenproof dish and layer the bread with the cinnamon-sugar and raisins. Combine the milk and eggs and pour over the bread. Bake for 40 to 45 minutes.

From left, Marian Kerley,
Brian Roughan, and
Noreen and Joe Roughan
at the Easter buffet.

CHAPTER XI

MEMORIAL DAY

Menu

Blackened Chicken Brochettes With Cilantro-Lime Butter
Shrimp and Beef Filet Brochettes With Sesame Marinade
Grilled Herbed Asparagus
Vegetables Grilled In a Foil Bundle
Grilled New Potato Salad
Grilled Coleslaw With Gorgonzola Dressing

Fruit Crumble

Outdoor cooking makes

the most of summer's first bounty

at a casual get-together

THE GRILLING BEGINS

There are eight houses in the North Fork community of Bay Oaks, and the families who have summered there for more than 50 years have developed a year's worth of traditions. Inaugurating the summer with a Memorial Day barbecue is one of them. For Sean Connelly, who generally hosts the party, the get-together is pretty much a ceremonial flourish since he's lived there full time for the last four years. And "hosts" is a generous term since the retired retail executive gets a substantial assist from Matt Kar.

Matt, who spent his boyhood summers in Bay Oaks getting into trouble with Sean's son, has also become a permanent North Fork resident. For 14 years, he has been the chef-owner of the venerable Jamesport Country Kitchen.

For the chef, the Memorial Day menu presents a special challenge. On one hand, the holiday weekend is the traditional start of the summer season, and lots of fruits and vegetables are de rigeur. On the other, the end

Matt Kar prepares blackened chicken brochettes on the grill.

of May is still early in the growing season, and much of summer's bounty — strawberries, corn, tomatoes — is weeks, if not months, off.

There is, however, one vegetable that flourishes in Long Island soil in late spring, and that is asparagus. For Matt, there is no question about how to cook it. "I don't know exactly why," he said, "but grilling changes the texture somehow, makes it taste even better." Matt thinks that grilling brings out the flavor of just about everything, so nearly every dish on his Memorial Day menu spends some time on the barbecue, even his gorgonzola-dressed coleslaw, which uses grilled cabbage, and his Italian-flavored potato salad, made with grilled potatoes.

In keeping with the everything-on-the-grill theme, Matt gave thought to a barbecued dessert. However, he settled on fruit crumble. Later in summer he uses strawberries, peaches and plums, but for Memorial Day he makes due with Granny Smith apples, supplemented with some out-of-season blackberries. "Hot, cold, the next day, with ice cream, without," he said, "crisp is always great."

At left, host Sean Connelly

Iced Tea

Iced tea is one of nature's two perfect barbecue beverages. But while it's beyond most civilians' abilities to brew their own beer, homemade iced tea is relatively simple. Really the only two issues to concern yourself with are: Should you use the same tea to make iced tea as hot? And is there a quicker way to make iced tea than cooling down an equal amount of hot tea?

First, the question of the tea. Tea connoisseurs contend that varieties containing less of the bitter substance known as tannin are the most appropriate served cold. The easiest way to ensure that you're brewing one of these good-when-cold varieties is to purchase a tea so labeled. If you must choose among specific varieties, experts advise, stay away from Indian teas such as Darjeeling and Assam and look for mellower ones like Ceylon.

As for methods, there is indeed a way to make iced tea more quickly than cooling down an equal amount of hot tea: Make a concentrate using 1 cup of boiling water to 4 tea bags, or the loose tea equivalent thereof. Allow to steep for 5 minutes, then dilute with cold water and serve over ice.

Blackened Chicken Brochettes With Cilantro-Lime Butter

MAKES 6 TO 8 SERVINGS

Matt Kar prefers chef Paul Prudhomme's Blackened Redfish Magic seasoning for his brochettes, but any brand of Cajun "blackening" seasoning will do.

1 cup (2 sticks) butter, melted
2 tablespoons chopped cilantro
Juice of 2 limes
4 pounds skinless, boneless chicken breasts,
   cut into 1-inch cubes
1 cup blackening seasoning
1 pint cherry tomatoes, halved
2 large red onions, cut into 1-inch chunks
16 bamboo skewers

1. Combine the butter, cilantro and lime juice. Set aside.
2. Dredge the chicken cubes in the blackening seasoning, shaking off any excess. On each skewer, alternate pieces of chicken with the cherry tomatoes and 2 or 3 layers of onion chunks.
3. Grill over medium-hot coals, brushing the brochettes with the cilantro-lime butter while they cook. Grill for 5 minutes on each side, or until the chicken is firm to the touch.

Shrimp and Beef Filet Brochettes With Sesame Marinade

MAKES 6 TO 8 SERVINGS

This is a delicious combination. The beef and shrimp marinate for only 5 minutes, long enough to give them a hint of Asian flavor, but not so long that the shrimp become tough.

1 cup peanut oil
½ cup soy sauce
3 tablespoons honey
3 tablespoons cider vinegar
2 tablespoons sesame seeds, toasted
2 cloves garlic, minced
1 teaspoon minced fresh ginger
3 pounds beef filet, cut into 1-inch cubes
45 medium shrimp, shelled and, if desired, deveined
16 bamboo skewers

1. In a bowl, whisk together the oil, soy sauce, honey, vinegar, sesame seeds, garlic and ginger. Set aside.
2. On each skewer, alternate 4 pieces of beef with 2 or 3 shrimp. Place in a roasting pan in one layer. Pour marinade over and let sit for 5 minutes.
3. Grill over medium-hot coals for 4 minutes on each side or until the shrimp turn pink.

Grilled Herbed Asparagus

MAKES 10 SERVINGS

If you can't find fresh oregano or thyme, don't substitute dried; instead, use more basil, or a mixture of basil and parsley.

50 spears asparagus, ends trimmed and, if tough, peeled
½ cup grated Romano cheese
1 tablespoon fresh basil, chopped
1 tablespoon fresh oregano, chopped
1 tablespoon fresh thyme, chopped
⅓ cup red wine vinegar
¾ cup olive oil

Place the asparagus in a shallow pan. Combine the remaining ingredients and drizzle over the asparagus. Grill over medium-hot coals until spears are tender and just starting to blister, 3 to 8 minutes on each side, depending on thickness. Arrange on a platter and drizzle with remaining marinade, if desired.

Marni and Brian Gallagher Jr. have dinner with their 1-year-old son, Brian III.

Vegetables Grilled in a Foil Bundle

MAKES 10 SERVINGS

Matt Kar often uses elephant garlic (it's huge, but mild) for this recipe, but regular garlic works as well. If you haven't got enough space on the grill, you can bake the bundle in a 350-degree oven for one hour.

2 bunches broccoli, florets removed and reserved,
    bottom 2 inches of stems discarded
2 medium zucchini, cut into ¼-inch slices
2 medium yellow squash, cut into ¼-inch slices
1 red pepper, cut into ¼-inch slices
1 large onion, cut into ¼-inch slices
1 head garlic, unpeeled and broken into cloves
½ cup (1 stick) butter
Salt and pepper to taste

1. Tear off 2 (3-foot) pieces of heavy-duty aluminum foil and make a cross on a large work surface.
2. Place all the ingredients at the center of the cross and gather up the ends of aluminum foil, bottom piece first. Wrap securely in additional pieces of foil to prevent juices from leaking, and flatten slightly.
3. Place the bundle over medium-hot goals and grill for 1 hour, carefully flipping halfway through cooking. Remove the bundle from the grill and place on a platter. Slice the foil open and serve.

Grilled New Potato Salad

MAKES 10 SERVINGS

The potatoes for this recipe should be at room temperature, but you can boil them the day before and take them out of the refrigerator an hour before starting.

30 medium red new potatoes, boiled in salted water until
    tender, then cooled to room temperature
¼ cup olive oil
3 scallions, chopped
1 large red pepper, chopped
¼ cup freshly grated Parmesan cheese
½ cup balsamic vinegar

Halve the potatoes, then dip the flat sides in olive oil and place on medium-hot grill for about 10 minutes or until warmed through and marked. Toss the potatoes with the remaining oil, scallions, red pepper, cheese and vinegar.

Grilled Coleslaw
With Gorgonzola Dressing

MAKES 10 TO 15 SERVINGS

Mixing in the herbs at the last minute helps retain their bright color and flavor.

⅔ cup olive oil, divided
1¼ cups soy sauce
3 tablespoons chopped garlic
⅔ cup red wine vinegar
¼ cup sugar
1 head red cabbage
1 head white cabbage
1 large red onion
4 tablespoons chopped fresh basil
    (or 2 of basil and 2 of fresh oregano)
½ cup crumbled Gorgonzola (or other blue cheese)

1. Combine ⅓ cup of the olive oil, the soy sauce and chopped garlic. Set aside. Combine vinegar, sugar and the remaining ⅓ cup olive oil. Set aside.
2. Cut off the base of each cabbage head, remove any damaged outer leaves and cut through the base, into 1-inch-thick slices. Cut the onion into thick slices. Place the cabbage and onion slices on the grill and drizzle with the olive oil-soy sauce mixture. Grill over medium-hot coals until tender and just starting to char, about 4 minutes on each side.
3. Roughly chop or slice the grilled cabbage and onion, then combine with the vinegar-sugar mixture. When ready to serve, toss with the basil and Gorgonzola.

Fruit Crumble

MAKES 10 SERVINGS

6 Granny Smith apples, peeled,
  cored, quartered and sliced ¼ inch thick
2 tablespoons sugar
1 teaspoon cinnamon
½ pint blackberries or other berries
For the topping:
1 cup flour
¾ cup sugar
1 teaspoon baking powder
2 eggs
3 tablespoons melted butter

1. Preheat the oven to 350 degrees. Arrange the apple slices in a 9-by-13-inch baking dish. Combine 2 tablespoons of sugar with the cinnamon and sprinkle over the apples. Mix well to coat the apples. Top with the berries.

2. To make the topping, stir together the flour, sugar and baking powder. Add the eggs and mix lightly with your fingertips or a pastry blender until the mixture resembles coarse meal. Spread over the fruit.

3. Drizzle the melted butter over the topping. Bake for about 1 hour, until the apples are tender and the liquid bubbles.

CHAPTER XII

FOURTH OF JULY

Menu

Lemonade

Cornell Barbecued Chicken
Gerry and Ralph Hulse's Coleslaw
Corn on the Cob

Marion E. King's Fresh Blueberry Pie
Old Steeple Holiday Squares
Very Vanilla Ice Cream
Sliced Watermelon

A church founded even earlier

than the nation throws its annual

Independence Day barbecue

CLASSIC AMERICAN FARE

Handsome, old, white clapboard churches still dot the landscape of Long Island's East End. They bespeak stories of early settlers and church picnics that were once held on their sweeping green lawns. Some of these churches existed prior to the signing of the Declaration of Independence in 1776.

Each year on the Saturday that falls just after the Fourth of July, one of those churches, the Old Steeple Community Church on the Main Road in Aquebogue, recalls those earlier times with a classic barbecue. The menu is as all-American as blueberry pie: slow-cooked, succulent chicken, corn on the cob dipped in melted butter, baked potatoes, homemade coleslaw, Parker House rolls, slabs of icy-cold watermelon, iced tea, lemonade and coffee. Though the white-shingled building dates to 1860, the church fellowship was formed in 1750, and the names of the first members, displayed in the vestibule of the sanctuary, read like a history of the families who settled this island: Wells, Reeve, Corwin, Moore, Terry, Youngs, though also sometimes given as

Opposite: From left, June Stevenson and Donna Doroszka

Young, Swezey, though there are various spellings of this family name, Howell, Luce. Descendants of many of these families still worship here.

The church, now as then, is in the midst of a farming community, said Rev. Robert Newton Terry, the pastor. In spring planting season, 7 o'clock Sunday breakfast services are held at farmers' homes. "It's our natural constituency," said Terry.

Most years, the first corn is just coming in by barbecue day, so the event celebrates the crop as well as our nation's independence. Corwin Duck Farm, just across the road, supplies the refrigerated truck that keeps food cold the day of the barbecue. George Reeve, a local farmer, supplies corn, cabbage, potatoes and watermelon. Edgar Goodale, who is in charge of the barbecue pit, has followed the example of his mother, Mary, and his father, Jesse, who have been involved in

church activities all their lives. Now, his own sons are learning how to tend the big barbecue.

Donna Hulse Doroszka and her husband, Joe, grate cabbage for coleslaw on an ancient wooden slicer, a chore handed down by her parents, Ralph and Gerry Hulse. Organization is key when feeding 500. The barbecue chairman inherits from past chairs a big looseleaf notebook full of lists detailing when corn-husking and butter-melting are to begin.

Fashions have changed since the church was founded. But it does not take much imagination to picture the lawn filled with long tables and with other men, wearing breeches and frock coats, and other women, clad in flowing dresses with cinched-in waists, their complexions sheltered by broad-brimmed hats. There is, however, an addition. A new flag is waving in the faintly salty breeze, and it is full of stars.

Cornell Barbecued Chicken

MAKES 10 SERVINGS, OR 300

The recipe used for Old Steeple's chicken barbecue comes from a New York State College of Agriculture Cornell Extension Bulletin written by Robert C. Baker, probably in the 1950s. We give a recipe that will feed 10. The amounts needed for 300 are in parentheses.

5 (150) 2½- to 3-pound chickens, halved
2 cups (5 quarts) cooking oil
4 cups (10 quarts) cider vinegar
4 tablespoons (4½ cups) salt, or to taste
1½ teaspoons (4 tablespoons) pepper
2 tablespoons (1¼ cups) poultry seasoning
2 eggs (30 eggs), beaten well

1. Build a fire about an hour ahead of time and let the coals get very hot.
2. Pull the excess fat off of the chickens.
3. For the basting sauce: Use a whisk and a strong arm to thoroughly beat together all of the remaining ingredients.
4. Place half the chickens on the grill, bone side down, skin side up. Cook the chicken about 10 minutes and turn. This is more easily done if you use 2 racks, with chickens between them, and have 4 people, wearing heat-proof mitts or gloves, turn the whole rack at once.
5. Baste the chicken with the sauce. An easy way to do this is with a clean, never-before-used watering can. (Or, for the smaller amount of chicken, you can punch holes in the lid of a mayonnaise jar and sprinkle the basting sauce from the jar.)
6. Continue turning and basting frequently for about 1½ hours for smaller chickens, as much as 2 to 2½ hours for larger chickens. Use less sauce at the beginning and more at the end of the cooking time; this will decrease the chance of the chicken burning. The chicken is done when an instant-read thermometer inserted into the joint between the thigh and lower leg (without touching a bone) reads 160 to 165 degrees.
7. If not serving the chicken immediately, transfer to a large, clean metal garbage can lined with foil, if making the larger quantity. Leave plenty of overlap on the foil. Wrap snugly in foil and put the lid on the garbage can. The barbecue team claims that this is part of the secret of tender, juicy chicken. Think of it as post-cooking marinating. If cooking the smaller quantity, use a large, foil-lined canning kettle to wrap the chicken in.

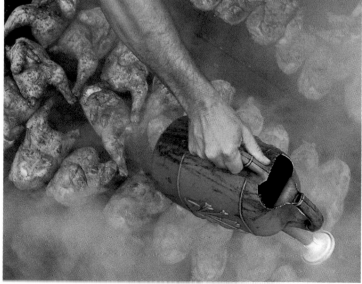

At left, Gary Young and his daughter, Isabelle, turn the chicken as it cooks. A watering can is used, right, to baste the chicken.

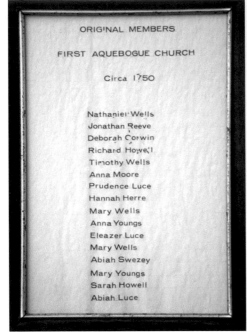

ORIGINAL MEMBERS

FIRST AQUEBOGUE CHURCH

Circa 1750

Nathaniel Wells
Jonathan Reeve
Deborah Corwin
Richard Howell
Timothy Wells
Anna Moore
Prudence Luce
Hannah Herre
Mary Wells
Anna Youngs
Eleazer Luce
Mary Wells
Abiah Swezey
Mary Youngs
Sarah Howell
Abiah Luce

Above, the names of the first church members are displayed in a frame. Right, Barbara ter Kuile serves picnicgoers while Joe Doroszka, opposite, enjoys an ear of corn.

Making Lemonade

A great lemonade trick is to gussy up storebought lemonade by thinning it with extra water to reduce the sweetness, then adding the juice of a fresh lemon or two. But nothing beats the made-from-scratch version, served with plenty of ice in a tall, comely glass. We like it not-so-sweet, but you can fix it to suit yourself.

Lemonade

2 cups sugar
1 cup water
Juice of 4 lemons
Water
¼ teaspoon pure vanilla extract, or to taste, optional
Fresh mint leaves, optional

1. In a saucepan, combine the sugar and water and bring to a boil. Let simmer for 5 minutes or until sugar is completely dissolved. This is a simple syrup.
2. Add ½ cup of the simple syrup to the lemon juice. Chill. (Pour the remaining simple syrup into a clean glass container and store in refrigerator. It keeps for weeks and may be used to sweeten other drinks, or more lemonade.)
3. Transfer the lemon syrup to a pitcher and add 6 cups of water. Add the vanilla, if desired. Taste for sweetness, and if you think it needs more, add syrup, to taste. If, to your taste, the lemonade is too sweet, instead add a little more water or the juice of another lemon. Serve over ice, garnished with fresh mint leaves, if desired. Makes about 6 servings.

Gerry and Ralph Hulse's Coleslaw

MAKES 10 SERVINGS

This is one of the recipes in the church's cookbook, "Recipes We Love." Cabbage should be shredded on a slaw cutter if possible.

10 cups cabbage, shredded
1½ cups chopped green pepper, optional
1½ cups shredded carrots
¼ cup chopped onion
1 cup salad dressing (such as Miracle Whip)
½ cup vinegar
½ cup sugar
½ teaspoon salt
¼ teaspoon black pepper

Combine the cabbage, peppers (if using), carrots and onion. In a bowl, whisk together the dressing, vinegar, sugar, salt and pepper, and pour over the cabbage mixture. Toss well.

Cooking Corn

The Fourth of July marks the beginning of a summer of sweet, long-awaited corn. In years past, said Jack Kratoville, a long-time barbecue worker, local farmers made special plantings of corn to be sure of having some in time for the Fourth of July fete.

The simplest way to cook it is one of the best: Boil it, then roll in a skillet of melted butter, as they do at Old Steeple.

A method we have found to be foolproof is this: Bring a large quantity of water to a boil, throw the husked corn in, put the lid on the pot, and turn off the heat. For very tender, young corn, 3 to 5 minutes steeping in hot water is plenty. For older corn, figure 5 to 8 minutes. To apply butter, some folks drag corn through a stick of butter that is used only as "rubbing butter" for this purpose. Others butter a slice of plain white bread, fold it around the corn, and use it as a buttering tool. Either way is easier than chasing a pat of butter that keeps slip-sliding away. To grill corn, pull husks back from the ears without breaking them and remove silks. Rub a little butter on the ears, pull husks back over corn and tie with a piece of husk or twine. On a rack about 4 inches above hot coals, grill corn for about 20 minutes, turning every 5 minutes. Have handy a spray bottle of water, in case husks catch fire.

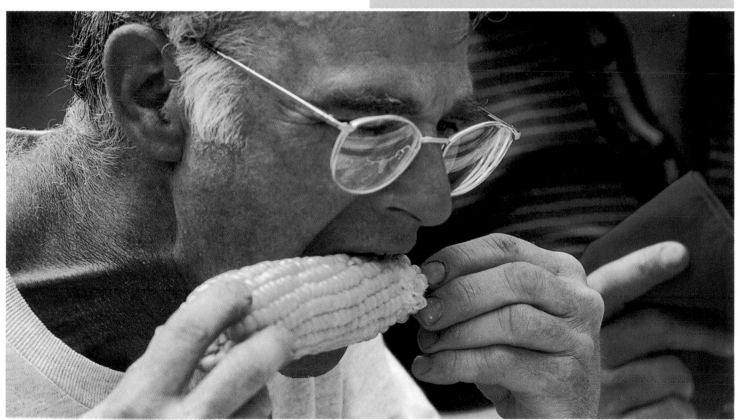

Marion E. King's Fresh Blueberry Pie

MAKES 8 TO 10 SERVINGS

Chilled watermelon is the finale to the chicken dinner, but at other church events, such pies as this go quickly.

5 cups blueberries, washed, divided
1 cup sugar, divided
1 cup water, divided
1 teaspoon lemon zest
3 tablespoons cornstarch
1 (9-inch) baked pie shell
Whipped cream, optional

1. Bring 1 cup of the berries, ¾ cup sugar, ¾ cup water and lemon zest to a boil in a saucepan.
2. Combine the remaining sugar, water, cornstarch and stir into boiling berries. Cook about 1 minute or until clear and thickened. Cool.
3. Place the remaining 4 cups berries in the pie shell. Cover with the cooled glaze. Chill until completely set. Serve with the whipped cream, if desired.

Old Steeple Holiday Squares

MAKES 20 SERVINGS

Several church women make these, and they are a sought-after favorite at the church's fall harvest dinner.

1 cup butter or margarine, at room temperature
1½ cups sugar
4 eggs
2 cups flour
1 tablespoon pure lemon extract
1 (21-ounce) can cherry pie filling
Confectioners' sugar, optional

1. Cream together the butter or margarine and sugar until light and fluffy. Add the eggs 1 at a time, beating well, until fluffy.
2. Stir in the flour and lemon extract. Spread batter evenly into a greased, 12-by-17-inch jelly-roll pan.
3. Lightly mark the batter off into 20 even squares. Put 1 heaping tablespoon of cherry pie filling in the middle of each square. (Use three cherries to each square if you want to make a cloverleaf pattern.) Bake at 350 degrees for about 35 to 40 minutes. Cool. Sprinkle with confectioners' sugar, if desired. Cut into 20 squares.

Very Vanilla Ice Cream

MAKES ABOUT 1 GALLON

A touch of brown sugar gives added depth to vanilla ice cream, a summertime favorite.

4 egg yolks
1 teaspoon salt
1½ cups sugar
¼ cup brown sugar
½ cup all-purpose flour
4 cups whole milk
1 vanilla bean, split
1 tablespoon pure vanilla extract
3 to 4 cups heavy cream
4 bags ice (if freezing with hand-cranked machine)
Plenty of rock salt (or kosher salt)

1. In a medium-large saucepan, combine the egg yolks, salt, sugars, flour and a little of the milk, to make a paste. Gradually add remaining milk, whisking or stirring to keep smooth. Scrape the seeds out of the vanilla bean and add the bean and seeds to mixture. Cook over medium heat, stirring constantly, until the mixture is thick, as for a pudding. Remove from heat and stir in the vanilla extract. If the pudding has any lumps, strain it. Cool, cover with wax paper so that pudding does not form a skin and refrigerate, at least 4 hours or as long as 24 hours.

2. Remove the vanilla bean from mixture. Transfer to the canister of an ice cream freezer.

3. Stir in the heavy cream.

4. Freeze according to the following instructions or follow the instructions that came with the freezer.

5. Place the covered canister of ice cream mixture, with paddle (sometimes called dasher) in place, in freezer bucket, making sure that the bottom of the canister is in its proper groove. Put cranking assembly on top, making sure that it engages properly and that the canister turns smoothly.

6. Place a layer of ice in the bottom of the assembled freezer. Break up any pieces of ice big enough to keep freezer from turning. Add a thin layer of rock salt, then more ice. Continue layering, ending with rock salt. The ratio you are striving for is about 6 parts ice to 1 part rock salt. Don't measure, just eyeball it. Bear in mind that the more rock salt you use, the faster the ice cream will freeze. But also keep in mind that when ice cream freezes too quickly, the texture will not be as fine.

7. Enlist turners. The ice cream must never be turned backward. Do not stop turning, or the canister will freeze into position. Add ice and, sparingly, rock salt as ice melts and the level of the ice and salt mixture goes down. (The freezer will have a plugged up hole; as water melts, you can uncork it and let water run out.)

8. While someone else is turning, assemble: a large platter or bowl, a long-handled spoon (wooden is fine), several tablespoons or teaspoons, rolls of wax paper and foil, and a clean dish towel.

9. When ice cream becomes more difficult to turn, it may be necessary to have someone stand or sit on top of the ice-cream bucket, to keep it stable.

10. When ice cream cannot be turned more by a strong person, it is done. Brush ice and salt away from the top of the canister so that none gets into the ice cream. Use a dish towel to wipe down the outside of the lid and the top part of the canister. Carefully remove lid and crank assembly, keeping canister in place. Be very careful not to get ice or salt in the ice cream.

11. Using clean hands that have not touched salt, pull dasher out of freezer, using the long spoon to scrape down ice cream into the freezer. Place paddle on large platter or in bowl and pass out smaller spoons to folks who are going to "lick the paddle." (This custom doesn't really involve licking, it just means spooning up the remaining ice cream clinging to the paddle.)

12. If using ice cream right away, scoop it out. If packing down ice cream for later use: cover top of canister with a double layer of wax paper and then a layer of foil. Replace top. Roll wax paper into a shape to fit hole in top of canister and insert it. Remove canister from freezer bucket. Pour ice and salt out into a dish pan or a large bucket. Pour water off ice and salt. Replace canister in freezer and pack ice around it. Add a layer of salt at the top and cover freezer with a burlap bag, a towel or a blanket. Set in a shady place or the basement. Let ice cream ripen for 2 or 3 hours before serving.

All About Watermelon

A Fourth of July without a cold, juicy watermelon is unthinkable. To find a ripe melon, knock on it with your knuckle. If the sound is sharp and high, the melon is not ripe enough. A dull, deep, hollow sound is more likely to mean a ripe melon. If the tendril or curlicue on the end of the melon is alive and green, it is unlikely to be ripe. The curlicue should be dry and brown. Watermelon is best deep-chilled. Lacking a walk-in cooling unit of some size, or a big space in your fridge, snuggle the melon in ice in a galvanized tin tub, a bathtub or even a clean garbage pale. To cut melon, said Jack Kratoville, who is charge of melon for the Old Steeple dinner, you need a long, sharp knife that can cut through a melon in one fell swoop. A shorter knife will make for a sloppy job.

There is one correct way to eat watermelon wedges: Stand in the yard, bend over from the waist, and let the juice and seeds fall where they may. Kratoville said that when he worked on a farm, "there was nothing like a vegetable or a fruit grown to its proper age, in the sun, on its vine or on its tree." When it comes to watermelon, you won't get better advice.

Opposite, top: Jennifer Boyle helps shuck corn before the barbecue. Bottom, a boy practices the art of eating watermelon.

CHAPTER XIII

LABOR DAY

Menu

Charlotte's Guacamole
Margaritas

Raw Bar of Fresh Oysters, Clams and Boiled Shrimp
Maureen's Remoulade Sauce
Mignonette
Cocktail Sauce

Steamed Lobster, Mussels and Clams
With Kielbasa
Corn on the Cob
Red Potatoes
Karl's Coleslaw

Fruit Pizza

A relaxed clambake

on a beach in Montauk

marks the passing of summer

A FEAST BY THE SEA

No culinary event is more evocative of late summer on Long Island than the clambake. And for good reason. By then, many of the foods that make up the feast are being harvested on the Island's East End. The local corn harvest is well underway, and the earliest potatoes are just coming in. Some summers, given the precarious nature of shellfish, even the main course, lobster, is being plucked from local waters. Labor Day, consequently, provides the perfect excuse for a clambake.

Montauk residents Maureen Tiongco and her husband Harry Theard observe this late-summer rite annually, and they do it the old-fashioned way: steaming a trove of mollusks and fresh produce among layers of seaweed in a rock-lined pit in their backyard. The seaweed is gathered from their yard, which opens onto Montauk Lake. The pit, situated near their beach, is a permanent fixture.

Maureen usually orchestrates the clambake herself, and counts on guests to help mind the pit and prepare food. On occasion she leaves the work to a professional such as Karl Vanston, the head of catering for Stuart's

Seafood Market in Amagansett who possesses all the qualities required of the clambake chef — patience, skill and an asbestos-like resistance to extreme heat.

If dinner is planned for five o'clock, Karl starts at noon, lining the pit with rocks and then piling it high with wood. "It doesn't matter what kind of wood you use," he explained. "You want something that's going to burn hot and fast. The point is to heat the rocks; the rocks are what cook the food."

When the flames die hours later, the cooking begins. Karl empties as much as 50 pounds of seaweed onto the embers in the pit. Next come the lobsters, the unhusked corn and red potatoes, the steamers and mussels and, finally, a couple feet of kielbasa. A blanket of seaweed covers all. Ninety minutes or so later, the tarp covering the pit is pulled back. The preliminary round of raw bar offerings such as littleneck clams and oysters give way to pit-smoked seafood and sausage.

Maureen, who used to perform in Broadway musicals, and Harry, a tenor who sang at the Met, couldn't imagine a more appropriate way to close the summer on the Island's eastern tip. "What makes Montauk so special is that it's so close to the open ocean," saidys Maureen. "You want to entertain? You have to have a clambake."

Stove-top Clambake

MAKES 6 SERVINGS

Most clambakes these days are pot-and-stove affairs, even for people who live in Montauk. Local laws restrict the digging of pits and the lighting of fires except on private beaches. This is what Maureen Tiongco does when serving a small group. Some fish markets will special-order seaweed for you, but if you can't find any, proceed with the recipe, and increase the amount of water to 4 cups for each pot.

24 cherrystone or soft-shell clams
6 small white onions, about ½ pound
20 pounds wet seaweed, with as much sand removed as possible
12 small red potatoes
6 live (1½-pound) lobsters
6 ears corn, unshucked
1½ pounds kielbasa, cut into 6 pieces
4 cups water
2 cups dry white wine
1 quart mussels, scrubbed and bearded if necessary
½ cup melted butter
3 lemons, cut in wedges

1. Cut 6 (12-by-12-inch) pieces of cheesecloth. Divide the clams, place on 4 of the pieces of cheesecloth and tie into packages with kitchen string. Divide the onions, place on the remaining pieces of cheesecloth and tie into packages.
2. Separate the seaweed into 6 equal amounts. Place 1 portion of seaweed in the bottom of each of 2 (18-quart) enameled pots. Divide and layer the clams and potatoes in each pot. Reserve 2 potatoes. Place another portion of seaweed in each pot and divide corn, lobsters, and onions between the pots. Cover with remaining seaweed and put a reserved potato in the center of each pot. Add the sausage pieces. Pour 2 cups of water and 1 cup of the wine into each pot and cover tightly.
3. Bring to a boil over high heat, then lower the heat to medium-high, being careful to keep the pots boiling. Cook for 25 minutes. Divide the mussels, add them to each pot, and cook for 5 more minutes. The clambake is ready when the potatoes on top are tender but not mushy.
4. Arrange all the foods on a large platter and serve with melted butter and lemon wedges.

At right, Karl Vanston spreads seaweed over hot coals in preparation for the clambake.

Opposite page: Top, Harry Theard and his grandson, Harry Kohut, gather seaweed in Montauk Lake. Bottom left, Lon Lauterio, a Suffern, N.Y. brewmaster, enjoys a raw clam.

Boiling Shrimp

Shrimp that will be eaten by hand, dipped in cocktail or remoulade sauce, are simple to prepare, mainly because they are cooked in their shells. If you want to devein the shrimp, make a shallow cut on the back of each shrimp and pull out the dark threadlike vein before or after cooking. Place the shrimp in gently boiling salted water until they turn pink, 3 to 5 minutes. Rinse them immediately in cold water.

To steam shrimp, place them in a basket over boiling water in a covered pot until they are pink, again, 3 to 5 minutes.

If you like spicy shrimp, add commercial crab boil to the water. When steaming shrimp, some cooks add ½ cup of white vinegar to the water for flavor.

Boiled and steamed shrimp can be served warm or cold. You can either let your guests peel their own shrimp, or you can do it for them beforehand.

Cocktail Sauce

MAKES 3 CUPS

This classic cocktail sauce suits raw shellfish or boiled shrimp.

1 cup ketchup
1 cup chili sauce
½ cup prepared horseradish
¼ cup lemon juice
2 tablespoons Tabasco sauce
2 tablespoons Worcestershire sauce

Combine all of the ingredients. Chill and serve.

Charlotte's Guacamole

MAKES 2 TO 3 CUPS

Charlotte Klein Sasso, Maureen's friend and co-owner of Stuart's Seafood Market in Amagansett, brought this guacamole to the clambake.

3 ripe Haas avocados
1 ripe tomato, chopped
1 small red onion, chopped
2 cloves garlic, minced
1 to 2 jalapeño peppers, seeded and chopped
½ cup chopped fresh cilantro
¼ teaspoon cumin
Tabasco sauce to taste
Salt to taste

Peel the avocados and mash lightly with a fork. Add the remaining ingredients, blending only until combined; mixture should be chunky. Chill and serve.

Shellfish Safety

Shellfish have a reputation as a risky food and while it's true that clams, oysters and mussels can be potentially dangerous, it's precisely because of that danger that they are strictly regulated. In reality, a consumer's risk of eating seafood from bacterially infected waters is slim. In the event of an incident, the contaminated bed is closed, and the shellfish harvested from the bed are destroyed.

For most healthy adults, raw shellfish are not a reckless proposition. When purchasing them, keep in mind a few guidelines.

•Buy from reputable, established fishmongers.

•Clams, oysters and mussels should only be bought and prepared while alive.

•Make sure the shells are tightly closed. If not, tap the shell lightly and the mollusk should close. If it doesn't, chances are the shellfish is dead and should be thrown away.

•For soft-shell clams, touch the rubbery neck that extends beyond the shell's edge. If it shrinks back or moves, the clam is alive.

•Discard any with broken shells.

•Smaller shellfish in general tend to be more tender.

•To store raw shellfish, keep it refrigerated between 33 and 45 degrees.

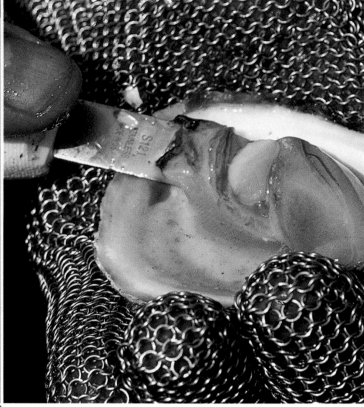

Mignonette

MAKES 1 CUP

Mignonette is a vinegar-shallot sauce traditionally served with raw oysters. Karl Vanston makes a gutsy version with balsamic vinegar.

1 cup balsamic vinegar
4 shallots, minced
2 teaspoons freshly ground pepper
2 teaspoons fresh lemon juice
1 teaspoon fresh lime juice

Combine all of the ingredients. Chill and serve.

Host Maureen Tiongco

Maureen's Remoulade Sauce

MAKES 3 CUPS

Maureen Tiongco's husband, Harry Theard, is from New Orleans, and early in their marriage he encouraged his wife to master remoulade sauce. Maureen not only uses this as a dipping sauce, but she spreads it on salmon before baking it.

1 cup olive or canola oil
2 large garlic cloves, minced
1 cup diced celery
2 bunches scallions, white and light-green parts, diced
½ cup Dijon mustard
¼ cup ketchup
1 (6-ounce) jar prepared hot horseradish
1½ teaspoons paprika
½ teaspoon cayenne pepper, or to taste
Tabasco sauce to taste

In a blender, puree the oil and garlic. Add the celery and blend until smooth, add the scallions and blend until smooth. Add the remaining ingredients and blend until smooth. Chill and serve.

Making Margaritas

The drink of choice at Maureen Tiongco and Harry Theard's clambakes is the margarita. "When you're tending the fire," said Maureen, "you've got to stay cool. Wine's too serious, and margaritas are cooling and festive."

Maureen has margarita-making down to a science. It's all in the lime you choose. Bottled lime juice tastes too artificial, she says, but fresh limes are "too much work." Frozen limeade concentrate, according to Maureen, makes the best margarita and the one that tastes closest to what you find in Mexican restaurants.

Here's how Maureen makes margaritas:

Into a blender, empty 1 large can limeade concentrate, 1 cup tequila and ½ cup triple sec or Cointreau. Add ice until the blender is filled halfway and then blend the ingredients. Pause, and fill the blender to the top with ice and continue mixing until the ingredients are well combined but the mixture is still icy. Serve in salt-dipped glasses. Makes 6 to 8 margaritas.

If you prefer daiquiris, substitute rum for the tequila. If you want strawberry daiquiris, just add some fresh strawberries.

Karl's Coleslaw

MAKES 8 TO 10 SERVINGS

How good can a simple coleslaw be? This good.

1 cup mayonnaise
¼ cup cider vinegar
2 tablespoons honey
½ teaspoon garlic powder
½ teaspoon onion powder
1 teaspoon celery seed
1 head cabbage, shredded
2 carrots, peeled and grated

Combine the mayonnaise, vinegar, honey and seasonings. Mix well and refrigerate. Ten minutes before serving, combine mixture with cabbage and carrots.

Fruit Pizza

MAKES 8 TO 12 SERVINGS

This is a perfect dessert for summer entertaining, according to Maureen Tiongco. It showcases summer fruits and can be made ahead of time.

1 (1-pound, 1½-ounce) sugar cookie mix
½ cup (1 stick) butter
1 egg
½ cup sugar
1 tablespoon cornstarch
Dash of salt
½ cup orange juice
¼ cup water
2 tablespoons lemon juice
1 (8-ounce) package cream cheese at room temperature
1 cup freshly whipped cream
Assorted fresh fruit: banana slices, kiwi slices, peach or nectarine chunks, blueberries, blackberries, raspberries, strawberries, grapes, pineapple chunks, canned mandarin orange segments

1. Preheat the oven to 375 degrees. Prepare the cookie dough with the butter and egg, according to package instructions. Spread the dough over a 12-inch pizza pan, and bake until light brown, about 20 minutes. Cool.

2. In a saucepan, combine the sugar, cornstarch, salt, orange juice, water and lemon juice. Boil and, stirring constantly, cook for 1 to 2 minutes. Cool glaze.

3. Beat the cream cheese until soft and fold in the whipped cream until creamy. Spread on the cooled cookie crust. Arrange the fruit in attractive pattern over the cream. With a pastry brush, paint the glaze the over fruit. Refrigerate.

At left, Maureen and Harry's grandchildren, Alexandra and Harry Kohut. Family and friends dine al fresco and enjoy the last days of summer.

index

the long island HOLIDAY COOKBOOK

Editor: Kari Granville
Assistant Editor: E. Clarke Reilly

Director of Design: Bob Eisner
Art Director: Joseph E. Baron
Photo Editor: Tony Jerome

Prepress: Newsday Color Services
Production: Julian Stein

Thanksgiving: Wendy Lin, writer; Bill Davis and Tony Jerome, photographers, and Joanne Rubin, food stylist.
Holiday Cookie Party: Wendy Lin, writer, and Ken Spencer, photographer.
Chanukah: Erica Marcus, writer; Bill Davis and Tony Jerome, photographers, and Joanne Rubin, food stylist.
Christmas Eve: Erica Marcus, writer; Tony Jerome, photographer, and A.J. Battifarano, food stylist.
Christmas Day: Wendy Lin, writer; Ken Spencer and J. Michael Dombroski, photographers, and Joanne Rubin, food stylist.
Kwanzaa: Joan Reminick, writer; Ken Spencer, photographer, and Joanne Rubin, food stylist.
New Year's Day: Sylvia Carter, writer; Ken Spencer, photographer, and Joanne Rubin, food stylist.
Chinese New Year: Erica Marcus, writer; Bill Davis, photographer, and Norman Weinstein, recipe development.
Passover: Wendy Lin, writer; Bill Davis, photographer, and Joanne Rubin, food stylist.
Easter: Erica Marcus, writer; Bill Davis, photographer, and Joanne Rubin, food stylist.
Memorial Day: Erica Marcus, writer; Ken Spencer and Bill Davis, photographers, and Janet O'Brien, food stylist.
Fourth of July: Sylvia Carter, writer; Bill Davis and Tony Jerome, photographers, and Joanne Rubin, food stylist.
Labor Day: Erica Marcus, writer; Ken Spencer, photographer, and Joanne Rubin, food stylist.